ADAPTIVE ANALYSIS

FOR
AUSTRALIAN
STOCKS

ADAPTIVE ANALYSIS

FOR AUSTRALIAN STOCKS

CREATING OPPORTUNITY
FROM PRICE ACTION

NICK RADGE

Wrightbooks

First published 2006 by Wrightbooks
an imprint of John Wiley & Sons Australia, Ltd
42 McDougall Street, Milton Qld 4064

Offices also in Sydney and Melbourne

Typeset in Giovanni Lt 10/14 pt

© Nick Radge 2006

National Library of Australia
Cataloguing-in-Publication data:

Radge, Nick, 1967-

Adaptive analysis for Australian stocks: creating opportunity
from price action

Includes index

ISBN 0 7314 0360 6

1. Stocks - Australia. 2. Stock exchanges - Australia. I. Title

332.6322

Cover design by Rob Cowpe

Cover images © PhotoDisc, Inc.

Printed in Australia by Griffin Press

10 9 8 7 6 5 4 3 2 1

Disclaimer

Disclaimer

This book is dedicated to
Beverley Radge
1939–2005

CONTENTS

INTRODUCTION

Adaptive Analysis for Australian Stocks is designed to help you question your current line of thinking and to show you an alternative way of looking at profitability and your own trading. My reputation in the retail marketplace is as a specialist in risk management and systematic trading strategies. While systematic trading may sound complicated to the new trader, it simply means a strategy that is defined by very specific rules — rules to define the trend, rules to enter the market, rules to exit and rules to manage risk. This is the way I have always traded and here I'd like to share my insights into trading the ASX.

I deal with technical analysis rather than fundamental analysis. It's my belief that the picture of a stock's current price action and price history cannot be disputed — it is a 100 per cent certainty. A company's balance sheet, earnings and disclosures, however, can be disputed. HIH, ION, OneTel and Sons of Gwalia are some better known and recent examples where many fundamental analysts got it plain wrong and, unfortunately, some investors paid the price for the poor analysis. Other examples are just as bad and I have been able to collect a huge amount in the early 2005 deluge of earnings downgrades. We can see the same trend of poor disclosure throughout the US with the likes of Enron, Worldcom, Adelphia and AIG — to name just a few. While an in-depth look at all of these examples is beyond the scope of this book, suffice to say I believe the reliance of many analysts on company disclosures is questionable.

I readily accept that the *application* of both types of analysis is equally subjective. In order to establish a fair valuation for a stock, a fundamental analyst must make assumptions on future earnings growth and other various contributing factors, such as the expected period of growth, non-growth periods and benchmark interest rates. Once these assumptions have been plugged into analysts' models, the resulting valuations vary considerably. These valuations are easily accessible by reviewing consensus data. However, the same applies for the chartists. The way one pattern is read can vary among analysts. In this area, I see technical analysis and fundamental analysis standing side by side.

However, the main benefit of technical analysis over fundamental analysis is that the charts provide a very specific right or wrong point where protective stops can be placed and losses can be limited. As you'll see shortly, the limitation of losses is paramount to the success of a trader and an investor, both financially and psychologically. People may be forewarned of situations such as the collapses of ION, OneTel, HIH and Sons of Gwalia by the deteriorating price action. Knowing when one is wrong using fundamentals, though, is a very grey area. Depending on the style of analysis employed, the lower a share price goes below its valuation may mean the better value the stock becomes. On the other hand, it may mean the valuation was incorrect to begin with. It's a hard ask for any analyst to amend his or her analysis and valuation in the face of a plunging share price — they are usually only forced do so after the fact and after the monetary damage is done.

At the time of writing, I have just turned 38 and I've been trading and investing since 1985 — a total of 20 years, or just over half my lifetime. I have personally traded almost every instrument listed on Australian exchanges and, quite possibly, every futures contract listed on the planet. In the early 1990s, I worked in the pits of the Sydney Futures Exchange. Later, in the mid-1990s, I worked in dealing rooms in

London and Singapore before starting a hedge fund in 1998. In 2001, with advancing regulatory conditions, I decided to move to Macquarie Bank where I became an associate director and managed accounts using systematic trading approaches built around technical analysis.

It was in the day-to-day dealing with retail clients at Macquarie that I realised the extreme psychological factors that play havoc with their actions. The need to almost always be correct, the inability to realise when analysis is wrong and then to take the appropriate action to defend an account, the fear of losing money, the over-reliance on unproven theories, or any mundane theory for that matter — all are products of psychology, and the list goes on. However, one factor clearly stood out above all others to create the most havoc — not understanding that profits can be generated regardless of what tools or analysis are used.

This book is about understanding this factor — that and how I go about doing it myself. In an attempt to not rely on the benefits of hindsight, many of the examples I use herein are happening as I write (June to August 2005) and are not yet completed. Therefore, after you've read the book you'll be able to reflect on my comments and assess the outcomes.

Unfortunately, my mother passed away earlier this year. This book is dedicated to her. Thanks to my father, my grandfather, Trish and the kids for being pillars of support during this sad time. I'd also like to thank those who have benefited from my insights over the years. As we've moved into an era of self-managed superannuation and personal responsibility for one's own financial affairs, it has always been pleasurable to hear how my analysis has made at least a small difference.

On a final note, remember — there is more to life than trading. The markets and the opportunities found within them will always be there tomorrow.

Nick Radge
November 2005

PART I

PHILOSOPHY

CHAPTER 1

AIMS

Your aim is to be profitable.

My aim is to help you *understand* how to make yourself profitable.

There may not appear to be a profound difference in the above statements, but let's remember that the vast majority of traders, and active investors for that matter, are losers — or, at best, marginal winners. Some people pay educators up to $20 000 to help them find an edge or the secret to generating profits in the markets. They listen to poor advice, perhaps from non-licensed practitioners, and rarely take any responsibility for their own actions. If you are like many other beginners, you probably already feel as though you've been through the ringer, trying many different methods and reading any book you could get your hands on. I call this the 'beginner's cycle' — moving back and forth between methods and ideas that just never eventuate into any concrete or consistent profits. It can be an expensive and long journey but, more importantly, it's an extremely frustrating journey that causes many to throw in the towel.

While finding a trading or investing style that suits you is important, it is more important to understand and accept why profitability occurs.

I say 'accept' because what I put forward here is usually dismissed for simplifying a so-called extremely complex concept. But simple works — and simple works through thick and thin, good and bad. (Of course, psychology is also extremely important; however, as I am not an expert in that field, I won't be exploring that side of the equation in too much depth.)

What I would like to do in this section is to realign the thinking processes that most likely operate within you. To start with I'll work through a few issues and hopefully get you thinking differently about them. What I'd like you to do as you read through is ask questions of yourself and those in the trading community you may have come in contact with. Rather than simply agreeing or disagreeing with my points, see if you can actually relate to them and understand the consequences of my arguments. Trading is about opening your mind to possibilities. After 20 years and seeing a lot, I am still learning, still researching and still passionate. Passion is the most important thing to develop — from there, profitable trading will flow easily to you.

Trading tools and indicators

Say we placed 100 consistently profitable traders in a room and asked each to discuss his or her trading style and techniques in five sentences or less. In my experience, it would be fair to say that while every person would use different tools and styles, every person would be trying to achieve the same goal — that is, generate profits.

Every time you speak with another trader (regardless of whether he or she is successful), every time you read a trading book, every time you receive advice, there will always be new information to take in — usually about an entry technique, or a new style, method or indicator. Everyone has an opinion. There are many successful traders — or at least people who have had just one profitable trade — and they have achieved this success even though they all use different tools and techniques.

Out of our sample of 100 consistently profitable traders, 40 may use fundamental analysis, 40 may use technical analysis and 20 may just use intuition or gut feel. Even then, the 40 who use fundamental analysis may use different aspects of that field. Some may rely on various ratios, while others may not take any ratios into account and rely solely on insider activity. The list and combinations are infinite. Of the technical traders, some will rely on moving averages, some on an RSI or other indicator, while others will rely only on price patterns and volume. Yet again, the pieces to the puzzle can be infinite. My point is that each profitable trader will use a different technique, style, investment time frame, information sources and tools. If all of the 100 traders are profitable through using different techniques, the common denominator cannot be the tools being used. It must be something else. Think about four profitable traders or investors who you know or have read about. Think about Buffett or Soros. Think Tudor Jones. Are they the same in their approach? Their tools, their time frames, their objectives? Of course not. So I reiterate, the common denominator must be something else.

If you agree with the above, it becomes easier to suggest that *it will not matter* which indicator, tool, time frame or software package is superior, and it's certainly not a tightly held secret or insider knowledge that makes them all profitable. All indicators, all technical analysis techniques, all fundamental analysis techniques, all software — everything you use to trade and invest — are nothing but tools.

The tools you use to trade do not maketh the money!

Let me use a simple non-trading analogy, shown in table 1.1.

Table 1.1: trading versus travel analogy

	Travel	Trading
Goal	Get from point A to point B	Be profitable
Tool	Car, Boat, Plane	Technical analysis, fundamental analysis, guess work

Our first non-trading goal is to travel from point A to point B. The tool to achieve that goal can be any mode of transport, such as a car or boat. As you are well aware, there are many kinds of cars and boats and when choosing one, our decision is largely based on our personality and financial circumstances. The same goes for trading. The goal of trading is to be profitable. The tools used to achieve this will vary depending on our personalities, financial situations, attitudes to risk and beliefs. Therefore, what you use to trade with are simply tools of the trade and not the reason why you will be profitable.

If you understand why profits occur, you'll be in a position to understand what tools are needed for you to achieve profitability. As a result, you may regret attending all those courses and seminars — or, better still, you may think twice about attending one in future.

The common ground among profitable traders

You may think that after setting aside the tools, there will be nothing left over. Wrong. There are two things — one is psychology, which will not be covered in great detail in this book simply because I am not an expert in the area; the second requires you to take a large step in your thinking. What I am about to say may rub many people up the wrong way. However, after 20 years of trading, the last seven of which have been spent closely involved with new traders, I believe what I have to say is accurate. It is certainly one of the strongest beliefs I have about this seemingly complex world of trading.

We're brought up with a huge focus on being right or wrong. At school we learn. We are then tested on that learning with exams and assignments. This continues all the way through our education — primary school, high school and at university. Right and wrong, black and white. It's ingrained in us from the word go. When we enter the trading arena, however, being right or wrong has nothing to do with being a successful trader and making profits. If you are like most people and believe that most important aspect of successful trading is being correct, unfortunately, it's only your ego you're caressing.

You can be a highly profitable trader and lose more often than not — indeed, some of the world's top traders lose more often than not. This concept, though, just doesn't sit well with most people because it's their belief that in order to be profitable you must be right. This line of thinking for an aspiring trader is very, very wrong.

Trading profitably is best understood when broken down into individual and simple pieces. Regardless of the complexities you build into your trading plan and routine, there is one constant underlying truth as to why you make a profit — the basic maths behind the result. All traders, regardless of how or why they trade, will need to understand this math, known as expectancy.

Expectancy as a term is probably nothing new to you. That may be the case, *but it is everything*. Alongside psychology, it's the common denominator among every profitable trader. It's not a fundamental ratio, a technical indicator or the Holy Grail. It's basic maths. The following question can make it easier to understand — would you prefer to risk $1 to make $2, or risk $1 to make $5?

The answer is quite straightforward — of course, we'd prefer to aim for the higher reward for the same risk. However, once the question of the probability of success, or accuracy of that potential outcome, enters our mind — that is, the possibility of actually being wrong — we tend to change the way we think. We revert back to our core beliefs of right and wrong. Because we are required to be right in order to achieve the reward, we then start thinking that we could be wrong — and so lose money as well — and it becomes a difficult issue to deal with.

Figure 1.1 shows a visual representation of the expectancy curve. This curve is made up of two core elements — the win percentage and the win/loss ratio. The win percentage is self-explanatory and simply means the accuracy of your trading. The win/loss ratio is calculated as the average profitable trade divided by the average losing trade. If after 20 trades the average winner is $200 and the average loser is also $200, the ratio is 1:1. If the average win is $400 and the average loss is $200, the ratio is 2:1. The goal is obviously to be in the upper portion of the graph shown in figure 1.1 — or the positive expectancy, and therefore profitable, area. Most people find they hug the dividing line between profitable and unprofitable trading and, as a result, spend their time alternating between being a marginal winner and a marginal loser. (Just as a side note, and regardless of how important you think it is, no manner of money management will save you if you operate on the negative expectancy side of the curve.)

Figure 1.1: the expectancy curve — the bottom line

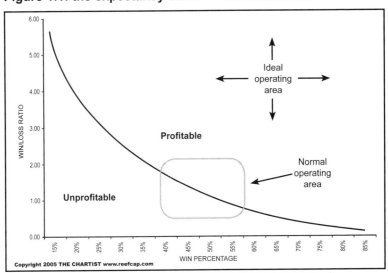

This alternating between marginal winning and losing is what causes us to continue to search for a better method. When the normal variance of returns takes us below the line, we tend to get nervous and drop the method, or add more indicators in an attempt to increase the winning percentage. This is our ingrained learning coming back into the equation and is the beginner's cycle operating. The thought *'there must be a better way'* always comes back to haunt us. As soon as we think we've found a better way, we slip back below that line and so start the process all over again. The correct course of action, however, is to allow more room for error. Our aim should be to create a method that falls deep within the top section of the curve, well above the line rather than hugging it. That way we won't get nervous when the normal variance of returns takes us below the line.

It is important to remember that no method can be correct all of the time. Every investment instrument — property, shares, trading systems or whatever — will go through periods of growth (generating profits) and consolidation (treading water). Card counters at the blackjack tables also have the same issues. Markets are dynamic. They change their spots whenever they feel like it and as such no method can dynamically change with them. To continue to search for a method that is consistently right will simply be an exercise in frustration and wasted energy. In order to trade deep in the upper expectancy area, an experienced trader will concentrate on the win/loss ratio, not the winning percentage (or accuracy).

I recently watched an infomercial advertising one of Australia's well-known investment newsletters. They claimed an accuracy of 73 per cent with an average profit of 10.3 per cent per recommendation. Obviously, the company hoped that this would encourage people to think they would make money by following the tips and should therefore subscribe to the market letter. What the company failed to mention was how much on average they lose on the other 27 per cent of their recommendations. Is this 'slight' oversight not a prime ingredient in the expectancy curve? Of course it is. If their average loss on those wrong recommendations exceeded 27 per cent, they would be net losers. I don't remember them mentioning that part, though. Clearly, they're playing up to the ingrained right/wrong psychology that manifests itself in less experienced traders.

I am far from arrogant in terms of my skills as a stock picker. My line of thinking is that I am no better than a coin toss. I am no better than random — that is, I have no better chance of getting a winning trade more than 50 per cent of the time. That may sound harsh, and you may be thinking that the four years you spent at university must make you better than random. To me, however, it is irrelevant. My discussion here is not one about random trading or the merits of not making a conscious decision to place a trade. What is most important is to shift the focus away from accuracy and toward the win/loss ratio, because that's the only way to really move into the deeper area of the expectancy curve.

The win/loss ratio

Here is a small exercise you can try with an Excel spreadsheet.

Enter the following formula in cell A2:

=rounddown(rand()*10,0)

Copy this formula down column A. (You can continue this as far as you wish to, but more than 1000 is certainly better than 100.)

In cell B2 enter:

=if(A2<5,(rounddown(rand()*10,0)),-1)

Again, copy this down column B aligned with column A.

In cell B1 we need the total of all the numbers in column B. I will assume you have copied down a considerable way, so use this formula in cell B1:

=sum(B2:B1000)

Now repeatedly press the F9 key while watching the number in cell B1. It will never be a negative.

Let's discuss what all this means. Very simply, the formula asks the computer to select a random number between zero and nine. Every time you hit F9, the computer will again calculate another random number for you. If that number is more than four (that is, five, six, seven, eight or nine) the computer will then assign '-1' to that cell. This '-1' means a one-unit loss to our trading — every time we have a loss, we lose one unit of our capital. A loss will usually always be the same amount, as long as we always apply appropriate risk management to our trading. (I say usually because there are certain times where prices may gap through a protective stop.) Risk management will be discussed in more depth later in this book.

To any number that was less than five (that is, zero, one, two, three or four) the computer then assigns yet another random number. This assignment represents a profitable unit to any of those numbers and that profit can be anywhere between zero and nine units.

So we have a scenario that will produce a fifty-fifty chance of a loss or a win. We control the loss by limiting it to a single unit, and when we make a profit we limit it to nine units in this exercise (this is only for our exercise — in the real world, there are no limitations on profits).

As long as we allow this pattern to be repeated over the long term, it can never create a negative number or a loss. Clearly, I have not accounted for trading expenses such as commissions or slippage; however, the theory stands nonetheless.

The average win and the average loss of your trading are directly related to the win percentage. Profitable trading will *only* emerge when the trader aligns these basic attributes to get a positive expected result.

Win/loss ratio versus percentage of profitable trades

Perhaps you're thinking I'm not that smart or that I haven't thought things through enough — surely if I had, I could win more often than 50 per cent of the time. However, after many years of computer simulation, real trading and reading almost everything written on the topic, the same conclusion always comes forward — maximise the winners, minimise the losers.

Below I test the theory again, this time with a basic trading system. The idea here is that if simple concepts are used, the results will always revert to random — that is, a win percentage of somewhere around 50 per cent. But before I do that, ask yourself how many fund managers you think actually beat the benchmark index. According to Vanguard[1], for the seven years to December 2004, the median Australian fund manager was unable to beat the benchmark in any investment sector — including cash. What this suggests to me is that

1   Vanguard Investments Australia *Understanding Indexing*, using Mercer data.

mediocrity eventually becomes normal. Many fund managers, even with their complicated trading systems, eventually revert to the index and therefore don't add any value — essentially, they're hugging the expectancy curve. They'll only make money if the benchmark index makes money, and they'll also lose money when the index loses money. How often do you hear a comment from a fund manager such as, 'We had a good year. Our benchmark index lost 10 per cent and we only lost 5 per cent'?

Let's use a trading software program (in this case, TradeStation) to generate a basic simulation. I have selected the price movements of the S&P/ASX 200 Index (XJO) for the period of April 2000 through to August 2005. During this time, the index increased in value by 41.5 per cent. I then told the computer to buy at the open of every single day — all 1353 of them — and sell on the close each night. Obviously, this method created a profit, as the trend was certainly up during that time; however, of interest was the winning percentage or the number of days the index was up compared to how many days it was down. This percentage is shown in the following results:

- total net profit $16.56
- gross profit $169.03
- gross loss   ($152.64)
- total number of trades   1353
- **per cent profitable**   **53.66%**
- number of winning trades   726
- number of losing trades   627
- **ratio average win/average loss**   **0.96**
- maximum consecutive winners   11
- maximum consecutive losers   8
- maximum intraday drawdown   ($12.02)
- profit factor   1.11

- maximum number of contracts held   18
- account size required $12.02
- return on account   137.84%.

During this five-year bull period, 726 days closed above the open and 627 closed below — or 53.66 per cent were up days. The win/loss ratio is 0.96 or, for argument's sake, 1:1. What this is saying is that all the net profits were made by just a very small percentage of the total days — just 99 out of the 1353. That's a lot of peripheral work to find those profitable days.

If you go back to the expectancy curve in figure 1.1, the results of this very basic test can be plotted right in the middle of the box that's hugging the curve. As such, any small variation in market conditions could take you below that curve at any time. Remember also that I have not included commissions, which would dilute the profitability considerably. While small mathematical edges can make a great system, you need a lot of patience, a lot of capital and a very cheap commission rate to fully take advantage of them.

A lot of people, because they are human and believe that they are smarter than the market, will see a 53 per cent profitability rate and try to tweak the entries and exits to create a better profitability. This is normal — and you could spend the rest of your natural life doing it. So let's speed the process up for you so you can actually enjoy your life.

Let's say that we'll only buy the S&P/ASX 200 if the Dow Jones was up the prior night. The easiest way to roughly simulate this is to buy if the open of the XJO is above the previous day's closing price, because usually Australia will follow the lead of the US market. However, we'll also make our system a little more sophisticated, because we notice that the market tends to go up for a few days at a time, then down for a few days at a time. Because of this simple cycle, we'll buy and hold for a few days instead of getting out immediately. Again, TradeStation was used to generate the results for this trading simulation.

The results were as follows:

- total net profit $0.76
- gross profit $1.52
- gross loss   ($0.76)
- total number of trades   94
- **per cent profitable**   **73.40%**
- number of winning trades   69
- number of losing trades   25
- **ratio average win/average loss**   **0.72**
- maximum consecutive winners   11
- maximum consecutive losers   4
- maximum intraday drawdown   ($0.23)
- profit factor   1.99
- maximum number of contracts held   1
- account size required $0.23
- return on account   328.32%.

The win rate is over 73 per cent. Now this may refute my random theory, but look what happens to the win/loss ratio — it goes down. If you look back at the expectancy curve in figure 1.1, you can see where these numbers fall. We've moved up the curve a little, but we're still hugging that line. Also of interest in these two examples is that while we've managed to increase the accuracy to 73 per cent, we've decreased the net profitability by a whopping 95 per cent (from $16.56 to $0.76). Apart from wasting time, what exactly have we achieved? We have achieved a level of comfort for our right/wrong mentality, but paid for it with a large proportion of our profits. I trade for profit. I don't care for the accuracy. What this tells me is that I should trade for the greater profit, but be prepared for the bad times when they come along. As opposed to not wanting any bad times, I just want to be profitable.

I could fill this whole book with similar examples to the above. We could make our systems more and more complicated to help improve those numbers and, hopefully, profitability; however, the more you attempt to improve the numbers by tweaking the entries and exits, the more you adapt your approach to historical price movements. This is called data mining and it is a very serious trap for new traders — and even more experienced traders.

Data mining relies on the benefit of hindsight. It means you have adapted your system to the market conditions of the past and, as we know, the market will never exactly repeat itself. As a result, even if it can be shown that a system would have been great in the past, it will not necessarily be worthwhile or profitable in the future.

There are several well-known authors preaching the back-testing concept, and there are certainly myriad vendors selling systems that seem astounding when tested, but that collapse in the real world. We need a method that will work in varying market conditions and economic cycles. The catch is that such a method is in the maths, not the tools.

In summary:

1   Everyone can profit in the markets, regardless of their tools.

2   Profits are derived from understanding the concept of positive expectancy.

3   Attempting to be correct more often than not does not necessarily make you more profitable.

4   The amount you win when you win versus the amount you lose when you lose is more important than trying to be right.

5   Be wary of infomercials and data mining!

CHAPTER 2

SKEWING THE NUMBERS TO WIN

Theory is great, but let's look at practical ways to increase profitability and move deeper into that profitable area on the expectancy curve. To do this, you must increase the win/loss ratio, or as I like to say, skew the numbers in your favour. There are probably many ways to do this but outlined below are a few simple ones that I use.

Low-risk entry

A low-risk entry means the distance between the entry point of the trade and the protective stop is small relative to another trade. The smaller this distance is, the larger the position size can be, as the risk remains the same. If you capture a successful trend with a larger position, the average win will increase with no increase in the initial risk and therefore the average loss will remain static. It really is that simple.

There are two ways to do this:

1   The first method is to tighten the protective stop. By tightening the protective stop you can trade more shares for the same risk.

Empirical evidence of this can be easily created with a computer simulation — for example, refer to appendix A and B, which show a crude computer test of this theory. I simply told the computer to buy/sell at open, exit at close and test protective stop lengths from one point to 50 points. Note that as the distance between the entry and protective stop is reduced, the win/loss ratio increases. I agree that having a one-point stop would be impossible in the real world, but the test is designed to show the impact tighter stops have on the outcome.

Apart from the win/loss ratio increasing, several other things also occur as the stop gets tightened. The win rate or accuracy decreases, the net profit and loss decreases, and the maximum drawdown decreases. (Maximum drawdown refers to the largest peak to trough dip in your account balance.) Importantly, the profit factor increases. The profit factor measures the mathematical comfort level of your trading and is calculated by dividing the total net losses into the total net profits. The higher the number, the better the method and the easier it is to trade.

The test shows that while the net profit and loss has declined, the risk has also declined — and at a faster rate, suggesting the low-risk entry creates a better risk/reward proposition. The better risk/reward proposition means you can regain the lost profitability by trading at a higher risk. What this means is that the journey of profitability is a lot smoother and, as such, you can trade with slightly more risk in order to regain the lost profitability without increasing the maximum drawdown. Instead of trading with 2 per cent risk, for example, you may opt to trade with 3 per cent risk.

So what is more profitable — a low win percentage (accuracy) with a higher win/loss ratio, or a high win percentage (accuracy) with a low win/loss ratio? The answer is the former. A lower win percentage with a higher win/loss ratio will be more profitable.

2   The second way to gain a low-risk entry is start with the
    protective stop point and work backward to the entry point. This
    means that, although you may identify an entry set-up, you need
    to pinpoint the protective stop point first. Once you have done
    this, ensure the entry point falls within the low-risk criteria.
    We'll discuss this important concept in more detail in chapter 3.

Breakeven stop

Being able to move the stop to the breakeven point as soon as
possible offers a psychological advantage because you can participate
in a trade that, theoretically, has no risk. More importantly though,
over time, the average loss will decrease if and when the breakeven
stop gets activated. This will naturally increase the win/loss ratio and
add further buffer to the expectancy curve. You might think that a
breakeven stop would increase the loss rate. It will to a point, because
as the stop is closer to the current price action you have greater chance
of getting stopped out due to day-to-day price gyrations. But it also has
an important psychological role to play. It stops hope from entering
your trading. You should never hope that a trade will come good —
the trade will either go in your favour immediately or it won't. If it
doesn't, you need to take defensive action.

Here are two simple guidelines that I use to apply a breakeven stop:

- Move the protective stop to breakeven if the position moves
  in your favour by 1.5 times to two times the initial risk. For
  example, if the initial risk on the trade was $400, move the
  stop to breakeven when the unrealised profit is between $600
  and $800. While you may occasionally get stopped out at
  breakeven as the market reverses, having your breakeven stop
  at this point will decrease the average losing trade and therefore
  increase the win/loss ratio. Further, if you have the trade entry
  point correct, prices should not reverse that far.

- Make the market prove your position through prices moving
  in your favour. If they don't, move the stop toward breakeven

after a few days. Don't hope — there is no point allowing a position to wallow around your entry price. If you do allow the market some scope and so leave the initial stop where it is, you are starting to hope it will eventually move in your favour. It is often said that a great trade will move in your favour immediately. If it doesn't, get out, decrease the loss (and therefore the average loss), reassess and try again. By doing this, you're keeping your losses down and not wasting your time waiting for a trade to come good. I'd rather take four $100 losses rather than one $400 loss — that way, I get four times the opportunity to make a big win without any additional risk.

Capture a bigger trend

One of the most difficult aspects of trading is giving back open profits — that is, giving back unrealised profits as the markets move against you. However, the more you can withstand it, the larger the trend you will be able to capture and, in turn, the greater the average win will be for an initial limited risk. The fear of losing unrealised profits — and so selling too soon — is possibly the biggest failing of new traders.

No-one knows if prices will move up or down tomorrow. Remember the simulated test we did in chapter 1 where we bought each day on the open and exited at the close? The win rate was 53 per cent, which proves that on any given day the market might finish up or it might finish down. If this is extrapolated out to when you're riding a position, on any given day the chances are that the position will either keep going in your favour or it won't. Therefore, to be scared of giving back open profits makes no sense — you're only thinking about one scenario out of a possible two. Thinking like this is not only illogical, it's emotional. It suggests you are placing more emphasis on the current profit than the potential profit if the trend continues in your favour. Concentrate on the next 1000 trades, not just the immediate one.

To take advantage of the trend while also protecting profits, we can apply the first two rules above — a low-risk entry and the breakeven stop — and then use a variety of trailing stop techniques. A trailing stop enables you to move your stop up behind the market price and so protect profits as the market moves in your favour. A trailing stop using a moving average is what I find the simplest and most robust. A wide trailing stop will enable substantially more trend to be captured; however, if this type of stop is used, more short-term market noise needs to be withstood and it may mean giving back large open profits.

Length of the moving average trailing stop

My experience suggests most people can withstand a moving average (MA) style trailing stop out to about 20 to 30 days in length. Beyond that, many people find it becomes difficult to remain focused on the trend because the open profits start to play a role. I use an 80-day MA trailing stop for some of my equities and futures models, and this can enable trends of beyond a year to be caught. Figure 2.1 shows the difference between using a wide stop and a tight stop. Markets naturally ebb and flow, so if you wish to capture large moves, the stop needs to be wide enough to allow these flows to occur. A tight stop will not allow open profits to be given back, but nor will it allow a larger trend to be ridden. If you are a serious active investor, you may use up to a 150-day MA trailing stop to capture sustained trends.

Figure 2.1: A sustained trend can be ridden with a wide stop

A computer can test the above theory. If we use a basic moving average breakout system where the entry/trailing stop interval is tested from 10 days to 150 days, as per table 2.1, it is possible to identify some important traits. The system was tested on News Corp shares from 1983 to 2004 and a $10 000 investment was used per trade. As the number of days used for the MA trailing stop increases (and therefore the profit potential compared to the initial risk increases), the win/loss ratio also increases from 3.08 to 14.87 and the average trade moves from $194 to $2221. The net profit moves from $25 998 to a whopping $73 308. Also note that the maximum drawdown remains relatively static and, again, that the profit factor increases. This example is not a one-off. Such trends within statistics occur across all strategies and time frames therein.

Table 2.1: moving average breakout system in News Corp

Length	Net profit and loss*	No. of trades	Win %	Avg. win/ loss	Avg. trade	Max. drawdown	Profit factor
10	25 998.60	134	38	3.08	194.02	–4589.02	1.89
20	54 624.54	92	35	6.06	593.75	–4589.12	3.39
30	60 225.46	67	49	5.18	898.89	–3259.00	5.02
40	52 940.99	64	40	5.62	827.2	–3828.68	3.85
50	46 147.82	61	39	5.01	756.52	–3213.69	3.25
60	43 772.43	59	35	5.87	741.91	–5083.92	3.24
70	54 391.86	52	30	9.67	1046.00	–4711.42	4.3
80	54 353.01	50	30	9.89	1087.06	–5432.54	4.24
90	53 819.65	43	37	8.36	1251.62	–5651.28	4.95
100	67 501.87	37	32	14.35	1824.37	–5085.54	6.89
110	61 651.54	37	32	11.94	1666.26	–5703.84	5.73
120	62 469.93	36	25	16.93	1735.28	–4734.19	5.64
130	59 704.24	31	32	11.85	1925.94	–4071.72	5.64
140	63 442.92	36	27	14.2	1762.3	–4544.20	5.46
150	73 308.76	33	30	14.87	2221.48	–4544.58	6.46

*Brokerage not included

Let's think about this for a moment. Imagine if you made 50 trades and out of those 30 were winners and 20 were losers (representing a 60 per cent accuracy). Each win was 1.5 times the loss. If you bet $1 on each trade, the net profit after 50 trades would be $25. The profit factor would be 2.25.

Imagine you made the same 50 trades, but this time you had just 20 winners with 30 losers (a 40 per cent accuracy). Remember that the win/loss ratio is directly related to the accuracy. Therefore, it is highly unlikely that your win/loss ratio would be 1.5 times in this example. Let's assume it will be three times, which is more realistic, even for shorter term methods. In this situation, the net profit would be $30, 20 per cent higher than the first situation, even though accuracy has dropped.

As at the time of writing, I have entered trades with win/loss ratios exceeding four times. This is where the money is made and it is common. Imagine if a system made four times the initial risk and was right 40 per cent of the time? The net profit would be $50, 100 per cent higher than the first example through being right less often! The equation is simple — most important is how much you win when you win, and how much you lose when you lose. Forget right or wrong. Think about expanding that profit compared to the initial risk taken. That's what it's all about. That's all that counts.

You can be assured of one fact regarding trailing stops and taking profits — you will never make a large profit by taking small profits. Allow yourself to run a minor profit into a large one. Don't think about the money — think about the process. Forget everything else, just try to get that win/loss ratio out as far as you can. If you can do it once, you will feel more confident the second time around, and you'll also start to realise the power of capturing a sustained trend.

Pyramid the position

When doing something right, do more of it. When doing something wrong, do less of it.

The above is one of my favourite mantras, and this is exactly the process that pyramiding follows. By definition, pyramiding is simply the process of adding to an existing position as the market moves in your favour. Pyramiding will expand the win/loss ratio because when a loss is incurred, it is on a smaller position; when an extended trend occurs, the position is added to so the trend is ridden with a larger position.

Say you place an order to buy NCP at $12.00 and the protective stop, according to your rules, is to be placed at $11.60. You would normally trade 1000 shares. In this situation, there can be only two outcomes:

- Scenario one — you get stopped out at the protective stop level at $11.60.

- Scenario two — you were able to exit the position using your trailing stop at a profit.

In order to analyse these two scenarios, we'll assume that in scenario two the trade was exited at $13.50.

Let's first review the outcome with normal trading — that is, without any pyramiding applied:

- Scenario one — if you were stopped out in normal circumstances, your loss would be $400 (1000 × 0.40).

- Scenario two — exiting the trade using the trailing stop allows a profit of $1500 (1000 × 1.5).

- Resultant win/loss ratio = 3.75.

Now let's review the outcome if pyramiding is used. When we pyramid, we buy a smaller initial position and only add to it when prices move in our favour. Let's assume that we'll divide the position into four parts, where we buy 250 shares at 10¢ increments as the price moves up:

- Scenario one — buy 250 at $12.00; stopped out at $11.60 for $100 loss.

- Scenario two — buy 250 at $12.00; buy 250 at $12.10 and move initial stop to $11.70; buy 250 at $12.20 and move initial stop to $11.80; buy 250 at $12.30 and move initial stop to $11.90.

- Exit position at $13.50, as per trailing stop, for profit of $1350.

- Resultant win/loss ratio = 13.50.

You can clearly see how pyramiding can skew the numbers in your favour — in the example above, the win/loss ratio moves from 3.75 out to 13.50. However, this is the best-case scenario, where the market moves in your favour without retracing. You should be prepared for the worst-case scenario.

In the above example, each time the position was added to, the initial stop was also moved up. This is imperative in order to keep the total risk aligned. The worst-case scenario will occur when we add the last position, in this case at $12.30, and then the market reverses and stops us out. The problem is that the stop is still at $11.90, which would result in a loss of $250. You may be fine with this, but looking deeper the initial position sizing was aimed at losing $100, not $250, so the win/loss ratio is reduced to 5.4.

Also to be taken into account is the extra brokerage incurred through multiple transactions when pyramiding — although, when a strong trend is ridden the resultant profitability, because of the win/loss ratio, will ensure brokerage looks after itself.

There are various ways to skew the numbers in your favour. Ultimately, it's a matter of decreasing the amount of each loss and increasing the amount of each win — and nothing more complex than that. When you put a trade on, it is important to think about the way you can reduce the risk. You cannot control the profits — only the market can do that. However, you can control your losses and, therefore, you can control your average loss. Be pro-active in your trade management. If you can get the average win/loss ratio out beyond 4:1, you will be a very, very successful trader — regardless of what tools you use.

CHAPTER 3

ENTRIES, FREQUENCY AND MIND-SET

Chapter 2 discussed the primary ingredient of profitable trading — getting that average win/loss ratio as large as possible. To do this, the first step is to limit the initial losses as much as possible. The initial loss is like a business expense. It's a necessary risk — you cannot trade without some type of initial risk. One way to get the win/loss ratio out as far as possible is to just trade low-risk entries. This concept is the cornerstone of my trading and you should certainly investigate incorporating it into your philosophy as well.

Selecting the low-risk trades

Several years ago, I tried a straightforward computer test using a basic break-out model. (As you may have gathered, I like to test my theories using an unbiased tool such as a computer. I have learnt never to make assumptions, personal or otherwise, when it comes to risking money.) The question I had on this occasion was, 'Should I take every entry that comes along, or wait just for lower risk entries?' I initially told the computer to take every buy signal between the entry point and protective stop, regardless of risk size. If this distance created too much risk, though, I told the computer to still take the trade but override the technical protective stop with a hard dollar stop (that is, a stop derived by a dollar loss rather than some other criterion such as a chart level). The results are recorded in table 3.1 and labelled 'Raw'.

Next I told the computer to take the same signals *but only* if the distance between the entry point and protective stop was within my specified risk tolerance. In other words, if the distance from the entry point to the protective stop wasn't within my risk tolerance (and therefore could not be considered a low-risk trade), don't just use a hard dollar stop, don't even take the trade at all. The results from applying this filter are also shown in table 3.1.

Table 3.1: all trades ('Raw') versus low-risk trades ('Filtered')

	Raw	Filtered	Change
Net profit and loss ($)	25 918	29 878	+15%
Max. drawdown ($)	–3 082	–2 990	–3%
Profit factor	3.09	4.71	+52%
No. of trades	51	41	–19%
% win	49%	59%	+20%
Average win ($)	508	728	+43%

As can be seen from table 3.1, it was better, in every category, to be more selective with trades — that is, to only take the low-risk trades and stand aside from the higher risk trades altogether. Net profitability went up by 15 per cent. The losing equity streak or maximum drawdown decreased by 3 per cent. The profit factor (dollars won divided by dollars lost) increased by a whopping 52 per cent. Remember that this statistic measures 'comfort' level, so we can also assume that taking lower risk trades results in a more comfortable trading experience. The actual number of trades I had to make declined by 19 per cent (less money paid to the broker is always good) and the amount of times I was profitable also increased by 20 per cent — not that this is important. The average win increased by 43 per cent, which can only mean the average loss must have decreased. As mentioned, the results came from testing my theory on the computer, which rarely lies. This is why it is instrumental in my analysis or testing of theories.

Tightening the protective stop

What exactly does a low-risk entry look like? Take a look at figure 3.1.

Figure 3.1: large range and ascending triangle in ANZ

Figure 3.1 shows a clear sideways trading range between $19.47 and $20.95. Prior to this, the trend was conclusively up, so *usually* the safest trade is to buy the breakout if prices pass through the high — in this case, at $20.95, marked as (1) — and assume the trend should continue. After entering, there are two obvious technical points to place the protective stop.

The first point is below the bottom of the range — in this case, at $19.47, marked as (2). The risk here is $1.48 ($20.95 – $19.47). If you were to risk $2000 of your capital to buy ANZ at this price, you could buy 1351 shares ($2000 ÷ $1.48). Therefore, if you bought the breakout and then got stopped out at $19.47, you'd lose $2000.

The next possibility for the protective stop is the minor pivot point — in this case, at $20.11, marked as (3). The trend here could be seen as an ascending triangle pattern instead of the sideways range. Using this stop would make the risk $0.84 ($20.95 – $20.11) should you be stopped out. Using the same risk allocation of $2000 of capital, you could now buy 2380 shares.

This is textbook stuff, so let's just stop for a moment and assess the obvious. After entry we will have absolutely no idea whether this trade will turn out to be a win or a loss. Regardless of how smart you think you are, it's impossible to know the outcome. All we can be certain of is that if we follow our plan and get stopped out we'll lose $2000, hence the importance of protective stop loss orders and executing them without fail.

The amount of dollars risked is the same in both scenarios — what is different is the size of each position. If this trade is a winner, which position do you think will make more money? Of course, position two, with the larger holding of 2380 shares, will generate more profits — even though the risk for the two positions was the same. All we've done is tighten the stop to allow a larger position size (2380 shares versus 1351) to be placed.

Let's assume we exit the trade at $23.75. Position one will make a profit of $3782 ($2.80 × 1351 shares). The risk/reward or the win/loss ratio in this case would be 1.89 ($3782 ÷ $2000). Position two will show a profit of $6664 ($2.80 × 2380) and therefore will have a win/loss ratio of 3.33 ($6664 ÷ $2000).

You can see that we have effectively skewed the numbers in our favour by simply tightening the stop. Imagine if we could have cut the risk on position two by 50 per cent again. It's basic maths, basic expectancy, and it is that simple (and removes the psychological impact). Remember, though, that the tighter the stop, the greater the chances of getting stopped out. Your immediate reaction here might be to focus more on reducing the chances of being stopped out. This means you are more focused on trying to be right rather than concentrating on the potential outcome if the trade is a winner. It's essential to remove this ingrained urge (in fact, remove any urge that pops immediately into your head — they're usually wrong). As already discussed, over time the higher win/loss ratio will result in greater profitability and this is more important than trying to vie for a higher win percentage. Let's look at the same trend shown in figure 3.1, but in a different light.

Figure 3.2: small range and ascending triangle in ANZ

Figure 3.2 shows the *exact* same pattern, yet on a smaller scale. What will be the outcome here using the same scenarios? Obviously, the position sizes here will be even larger and therefore the win/loss ratio will also be larger, all for the exact same risk of $2000. Let's run through the numbers just to make sure.

We've bought on the breakout at point (1) at $20.85. We can place the protective stop loss at $20.11, and therefore buy 2702 shares ($2000 ÷ $0.74), or we can trade the smaller ascending triangle and place a tighter stop at $20.39. This would enable us to buy 4347 shares ($2000 ÷ $0.46).

Assume again we are able to exit at $23.75. The first scenario above shows a profit of $7835 with a win/loss ratio of 3.9 ($7835 ÷ $2000). The second scenario shows a profit of $12 606 with a win/loss ratio of 6.3 ($12 606 ÷ $2000).

Now we have four different scenarios with just two things in common. The first commonality is we could never have known ahead of time that the trade was going to be successful or that we'd be able to exit at $23.75. That's in the hands of the gods (not in the $20 000-a-course vendor's opinion), but we did ignore the 'right/wrong' factor. Secondly, the loss was always going to be the same on each of the four trades — we were going to lose $2000 regardless of whether any of the set-ups were wrong. These are the only two similar characteristics in all four scenarios.

The differences lie in the tightness of the protective stop, which in turn leads to a larger position size. If, *and only if*, the trade is a winner, we'll always be better off with a larger position size on the trade. Go back to figure 1.1 on page 8 and see where these win/loss ratios lie on the expectancy curve and note how we've managed to move deeper into the profitable zone. A win/loss ratio of 6.3 doesn't even register on that curve. With this ratio, you'd still be a winner if you just won 14 per cent of the time! I'd like to think that I'm a little better than 14 per cent.

Getting closer to the risk-free trade

It doesn't matter what we do, as long as the initial risk is as low as we can make it. To have no risk would be ideal, but that just cannot be the case when trading or investing. We can certainly help our cause, however, by starting the trade with a low-risk entry and then quickly following up by moving the stop to breakeven or at least reducing the initial risk by 50 per cent. That is the closest scenario we can have to a risk-free trade, and this is exactly how I operate. It's a remarkably simple concept and one that will work anytime, anywhere.

Would it have mattered to the bottom line if we'd used a slow stochastic to enter these trades? No. Would it have mattered to the bottom line if we'd used volume as a filter? No. Would it have mattered to the bottom line if we'd used six different indicators? No. Nothing matters more than understanding the win/loss ratio mentality.

All these things, including the patterns I have used in the examples above, are merely tools to achieve our goal of making profits. The patterns themselves don't make you a successful trader. The moving average crossover doesn't make you a successful trader. The RSI, stochastic, ATR double-hitched backflip twist doesn't make you a successful trader. All these tools are just for your comfort — a way for you to feel in control and as such allow you to participate in the market. That's okay. We all need comfort when placing a trade, but think about why you'd spend $20 000 to buy a trading course or attend a secret seminar.

Remember — what makes you a successful trader is how much you win when you win and how much you lose when you lose. It won't matter what instrument you decide to use to trade. The same basic trading principle can be used in every market in the world — stocks, contracts for difference (CFDs), futures and foreign exchange — and on every time frame from three-minute charts right through to weekly and monthly charts. The same expectancy will be required anywhere in order to be profitable. A lot of people use my consulting services. They approach me to specifically learn how to trade FX or CFDs or another type of instrument. They seem to think that there is a fundamental difference between trading one instrument and trading another. I can see no differences, except in terms of leverage, across markets. They all work the same. They all create the same opportunities of trend and consolidation and will therefore always present low-risk opportunities.

If you disagree, that's okay. But I challenge you to prove me wrong.

Trade frequency

If the above discussion on risk-free entries can be found to be true, profitability can be further improved by trading with higher risk or simply trading more frequently. There are some caveats to this concept, however, which I'll outline shortly.

Firstly, let's start with trade frequency. If being profitable is about increasing the win/loss ratio and you now know how to do this, the next step is to increase profitability by increasing the number of trades we do in any given period of time. If you can achieve an average win/loss ratio of 4:1 and do 100 trades per year, you can then increase your overall profitability further by doing more trades per year. Pretty simple — although most people will attempt to increase profitability through the frustrating exercise of trying to increase the win rate. Just do more trading!

There are various, including some extreme, ways of doing this. For example, an extreme trade frequency would be a scalper who trades 30 times a day in one market. (Refer to my first book *Every-day Traders* — Wrightbooks, 2003 — for real-life examples of this.) Scalpers find a very small edge and then exploit it as often as they can. They usually trade one volatile market that has high liquidity.

One step down from this extreme would be to look at short-term moves — say, two to five days in length — and trade, say, five to 10 different stocks at once (more if you have the time). Stepping down even further would be to trade out to 20 to 30 days, as I attempt to do, and track more stocks to increase trade frequency. Lastly, you could capture much longer term trends and follow up to 300 stocks.

The advent of margin lending and, more recently, CFDs means you are no longer restricted by capital outlay. As such, trade frequency can be increased quite dramatically. Obviously the use of leverage is a double-edged sword so one needs to practise sound risk management.

Caveats on increasing trade frequency

Trade frequency is important, but the caveats are:

- The higher the trade frequency, the higher the associated costs such as brokerage, data collection and time. Of course, the larger your win/loss ratio, the better your net profitability will become after these costs are deducted.

- The shorter the time frame, the less instruments you can physically monitor. Conversely, the longer the time frame, the more instruments you need to watch.

Increasing trade frequency helps increase profitability if you have a positive expectancy method for extracting profits from the market. Throwing darts or tossing a coin may *theoretically* achieve the same goal but they certainly aren't psychologically appropriate for most people. While I have made my arguments in the last section seem rather simplistic, what can't be oversimplified is the importance of having the right psychological mind-set to trade profitably and consistently.

My thoughts on mind-set

While an in-depth analysis of the psychology of a top trader is beyond the scope of this book, it is another factor that is paramount to success, so you should take the time to study it more. While the concepts of the win/loss ratio and expectancy I have covered so far are all-important, it is possible that you won't be able to implement these concepts if you don't have the correct mind-set. Too many people come into trading with preconceived ideas of what is actually involved and one of the most destructive forces on a new trader is the emotional baggage brought to the table. It is, however, extremely difficult to teach the correct mind-set — which is why I am only highlighting its importance here. While I have used a psychologist to help me with my own trading, it is not a quick-fix way to make you a more profitable trader. The correct mind-set develops over time through experience and is certainly not something that can be taught in a $30 book, during a 60-minute consultation or through an expensive weekend retreat.

I realised a few years ago that my line of thinking is vastly different to that of many people I came into contact with. Previously, I had just assumed everyone thought of risk and expectancy in the same way as I did. While my concern for risk or having a losing trade was completely non-existent, or perhaps unconscious, it appeared to be a major dilemma for most people. It's not that it had never occurred to me that a trade could be a loser. I was very aware of the possibility of loss and also knew all too well my ability to string many losers together. However, I don't consciously get concerned about losing money in the same way as most people do. Perhaps after 20 years of trading and seeing everything from the 1987 crash to the implosion of HIH, it has become so second nature that now the thought of losing money sits deep inside my unconscious and has no bearing on my day-to-day decision making.

I view trading as simply entering a position and then defending the risk involved with that position. Defending the risk is about finding low-risk set-ups, moving the protective stop to breakeven as soon as it is appropriate and trailing the stop as the trend develops. In that mind-set, I simply don't think about the potential of a loss and I am completely free to accept what the market gives me each day. Unfortunately, this is very different to what passes through the minds of most people when they get into a trade. They tend to look for confirmation by reading a public bulletin board or even by unconsciously only accepting information that agrees with their position and rejecting information that conflicts with their position.

The market is not the enemy

Other people approach trading as if they are in battle and the market is the opposition. The market is not the enemy. It cannot hurt you. You can hurt you, but the market simply facilitates the buying and selling of the many and as such simply provides feedback via its prices. What you do with that feedback is up to you. If you don't use a protective stop, if you use too much leverage, if you do not allow the trends to be ridden, if you bog yourself down in too much analysis, you will lose money.

More often than not, most people blame the market for their losses and so create a 'me versus them' scenario. Many people have attempted to explain to me how the market is 'rigged' or how big players make it unfair for smaller players or how the broker issued bad advice. Ultimately, it is your decision to play the game and therefore your responsibility to ensure that you know what you're doing. You wouldn't attempt to fly an aeroplane without first receiving instruction and extensive training. Yet people who have no idea about how to be profitable in the market invest their hard-earned money in an arena that contains professionals who dedicate their lives to making a living from it.

Trading is not a hobby

Trading is a serious occupation; it is not a hobby. I do endless research on anything that might add to my trading and/or investing repertoire. In this day and age of leverage, we have the ability to extend funds across various strategies and we don't have to be overly exposed to risk in order of doing so. Too many traders stick to one single strategy or one instrument. While there is nothing inherently wrong with this, it limits their understanding of the markets and therefore their growth as traders.

Learn to be open to anything that comes along. I readily tinker with strategies or suggestions that I read about on chat sites, the internet or in books. On most occasions, the theory gets dispelled rather quickly; however, I have also found some gems. Because of this openness to ideas, I have been able to build on existing strategies and add new ones. This not only adds to my bottom line but also to my confidence in my ability to understand what is valid and what is garbage. I am able to very quickly decipher the difference between a good trader and an amateur just by listening to the way each talks and what each tends to talk about.

To get you started on the road to developing the correct mind-set, I would recommend *Trading in the Zone* by Mark Douglas. While it may take a few reads to comprehend it, it should help you to grasp the angle that I approach trading from. Your psychological fortitude plays an important role in all aspects of your trading and investing, so ensure you work on it. Your emotions will do everything they can to keep you in a losing position and get you out of a winning position. You are your worst own enemy and, generally, what you feel is the correct thing to do, is the wrong thing to do. Taking a quick profit may feel right, but it skews your ability to be a solid long-term winner.

Quite simply, you need to run a trend, not cut it short. You need to cut a loss as quickly as possible, not hope it will come good. I accept that you must find a style that suits you, that is comfortable and that you can replicate in the future. But going around and around will only add to your inability to make a decision and be a detriment to your bottom line.

CHAPTER 4
RISK MANAGEMENT

No trading book would really be complete without some discussion of risk management. I wasn't going to add this chapter, but after recently doing some talks it became obvious that many people still do not practise appropriate risk management in their trading. The topic of risk management, or position sizing as it's sometimes known, is paramount to your longevity as a trader. The bottom line really comes down to this — the more you bet on a single trade, the more volatile your returns will become. The more volatile your account balance is, the greater the emotional roller-coaster you will ride. Experiencing too many ups and downs, especially large ups and downs, is not really something that I'd suggest is appropriate for a career trader. It will create an unsettling environment in both your professional and personal life, and it may also adversely affect your health. It is therefore important to manage your exposure to risk and so create some trading and health longevity for yourself.

One of the simplest ways of managing risk is to simply divide your trading capital into equal parts. While this may not be the best way, it is certainly better than no way. I'll get onto what I think is the best way shortly, but for now let's just use the following simple analogy.

Imagine you are a professional golfer and compete on the pro tour. The tour events are made up of four days of golf and on each of those days you play 18 holes. In total, you will play 72 holes. As much as you'd like to play every hole perfectly, you know that is impossible. Therefore, while you simply attempt to play as best you can, the goal that is really in the back of your mind is not to have an extremely bad hole that destroys the entire round or tournament. In essence, you are managing your score by not doing anything completely stupid, like hitting bold shots or taking on too many risky shots. You attempt to avoid bunkers, play away from water hazards and out-of-bounds areas, and do your best to control the ball and keep it on the fairway at all times. You realise that if you fail to keep the ball on the fairway, you will be penalised harshly for the oversight.

When playing the tournaments you are also aware of external factors that may play a part in your decisions. Factors such as the wind, recent rain or dryness, angle of the fairways, speed of the greens and even the competition can have an adverse impact on your game. There are also external factors such as sports critics who may place thoughts in your mind or influence your line of thinking.

When faced with all these factors good golfers will simply take one shot at a time. They micro-manage their game by not thinking about the absolute end result. They simply play the shot they have in front of them. They play for safety and to stay in the game for the long haul. They play each shot so as to be in some type of contention at the end of the tournament, as you can't win if you're not in contention.

If we apply this analogy to trading, hitting a bad shot into a water hazard and being penalised is like taking a much larger loss than the average. We know that not every trade will be a winner, just like a pro golfer will know that not every shot will be perfect. But we trade to stay in play and by that I mean we only allow a small amount of risk on each trade. When we do have some bad trades, and they are bound to occur, they will not disrupt the end game, which is to have enough capital to keep on trading.

So think like a pro golfer and divide your capital into 72 equal parts — as if each trade you make is similar to each hole a pro golfer plays in a four-day tournament. A single hole cannot be responsible for winning the tournament, but a very bad hole can certainly make it impossible to win. Good traders understand that some trades will be losers, some trades will be winners and some will be great wins, but they do their best to ensure that a single trade or even a string of losing trades will not destroy their account balances.

The probable length of a losing streak

As long as you have divided your capital into 72 equal parts and placed a protective stop, a single trade on its own is rarely destructive. However, when a string of losing trades occurs it can be a cause for concern — both financially and emotionally. You might think that if you win about 50 per cent of the time, a winning trade would surely follow each losing trade. Nothing could be further from the truth. I remember waiting for a plane in Hong Kong several years ago and being bored. I started tossing a coin and counting how often a streak of heads or tails would occur — after all, a coin only has two sides and so there is a fifty-fifty chance of a head or a tail coming up. Mathematically I knew the outcome, but I wanted to see it for myself. Sure enough, on quite a few occasions I was able to toss a run of nine heads or tails. Runs of five were extremely common.

If you were able to mathematically ascertain the probable length of a losing streak, you could better prepare yourself for its potential impact — financially and emotionally — when it does occur. Using an Excel spreadsheet and our win percentage, we can make some assumptions as to what is possible.

For the purposes of the exercise, I'll use my humble pie example, where I expect to win around 50 per cent of the time. In cell A1 of the Excel spreadsheet, enter that 50 per cent expectancy as 50. In cell A2, enter how many trades you would like to test the theory on. It's best to be conservative, so a large number such as 10 000 is better than 100. Enter 10 000 into cell A2. In cell A3, enter the following formula:

=ROUND(LN(A2)/-LN((1-(A1/100))),0)

Once you have entered this formula, '13' automatically appears in cell A3. What this means is that after 10 000 trades with an average win rate of 50 per cent, there is a chance that you could sustain 13 consecutive losers in a row. It's always best to err further on the side of caution and expect that perhaps even worse than this could occur.

This gives us some valuable information, both mentally and financially. I say mentally because most people go looking for another method after about five consecutive losers. If you intimately understand what is possible in trading, both good and bad, you will be more inclined to see a losing streak through. Knowing what is possible also allows you to consider the emotional consequences that can pop up when your capital starts being depleted by a string of losing trades. What will your spouse say? Will you tell your friends? How will your mood be at work the next day? Will you have a few extra drinks at the pub that night? If you prepare yourself for 13 (or more) losses in a row, when the inevitable losing streak does come along, you'll be ready and know that it is just part and parcel of trading.

But this chapter is about risk, not psychology, so let's concentrate on the financial side of the equation.

Capital allocation

There is a well-known trading course sold in Australia that has been around for 20 or more years. The operators of this course suggest you should risk 10 per cent of your initial account equity on each trade. Is this wise? I say no. What happens if the first five trades are losses? They, obviously, will tell you that it won't happen, but what if you've just paid $1000 for this great trading course and you lose 50 per cent of your capital in just five trades? You'd be devastated. I say I am no better than random, or a 50 per cent win rate. Therefore, according to our spreadsheet calculations, there is a possibility I could have 13 losses in a row. In light of this, I cannot bet 10 per cent of my account on each trade because there is a chance I will lose more than what is in my account. Even if I bet 5 per cent on each trade, after 13 losing trades my account balance would have declined by 65 per cent. Is that acceptable to you? It's not to me. The students of the above course would have to achieve a minimum win rate of 60 per cent — which could still potentially produce 10 losers in a row, meaning there was still a chance of losing 100 per cent of the account. I never want to be in that position or even close to that position. If you are risking 10 per cent of your initial equity with every trade, an account decline of less than 50 per cent will only occur if your win rate exceeds 82 per cent. There are not too many traders in the world who can do that.

If we use our golfing analogy and divide our capital into 72 equal parts, we're risking just 1.39 per cent of our equity on each trade. (Remember — the amount risked is the amount lost if you are stopped out of a trade, not the total amount invested.) This means that 13 consecutive losers would cause a total loss of just 18 per cent. Is that acceptable to you? It certainly is to me. After making this basic calculation, we can adjust our risk on each trade to suit our own risk profile. Each person has a different risk appetite. Some people are more than happy to lose 50 per cent of their account balance. Others shudder at the thought of losing 20 per cent. Some of you may think that such a losing streak would not happen to them. Maybe not, but do you want to put yourself in that position? I'd like to be a fly on the wall as you explain to your spouse why you've lost 65 per cent of your capital in the first few weeks of your new trading career. Your friends and family will call you a gambler — and, unfortunately, if you bet too much on a single trade, that's exactly what you are.

Advanced asset allocation

This basic concept of splitting your capital into equal parts is adequate for a beginner or intermediate trader. If you wish to take the next step or you are quite conservative, the best method I have used is fixed fractional position sizing.

Fixed fractional (FF) also uses the concept of percentage risk per position but is calculated from the account balance on an ongoing basis rather than selected from the start. It is also very useful because it naturally compounds your account when you're profitable, yet defends it when you are having a losing streak. When using this method, a percentage risk of your account is chosen for each trade. As shown above, the higher the risk, the more you'll lose (or win) and the more volatile your account will become.

Assume your starting account balance is $10 000 and you risk 5 per cent on each trade. The first trade will have a risk of $500 (10 000 × 0.05). If this trade is a loser, the second trade will have a risk of $475. ($9500 × 0.05). If that trade is also a loser, the third trade will have a risk of $451. Each successive loss will make the capital go lower and therefore the percentage risk of that capital will also decrease.

Table 4.1 shows the equity decline for various risk percentages after 20 losers in a row.

Table 4.1: varying account balances after 20 consecutive losers

Balance	5%	Balance	4%	Balance	3%	Balance	2%	Balance	1%
10 000		10 000		10 000		10 000		10 000	
9500	500	9600	400	9700	300	9800	200	9900	100
9025	475	9216	384	9409	291	9604	196	9801	99
8574	451	8847	369	9127	282	9412	192	9703	98
8145	429	8493	354	8853	274	9224	188	9606	97
7738	407	8154	340	8587	266	9039	184	9510	96
7351	387	7828	326	8330	258	8858	181	9415	95
6983	368	7514	313	8080	250	8681	177	9321	94
6634	349	7214	301	7837	242	8508	174	9227	93
6302	332	6925	289	7602	235	8337	170	9135	92

Balance	5%	Balance	4%	Balance	3%	Balance	2%	Balance	1%
5987	315	6648	277	7374	228	8171	167	9044	91
5688	299	6382	266	7153	221	8007	163	8953	90
5404	284	6127	255	6938	215	7847	160	8864	90
5133	270	5882	245	6730	208	7690	157	8775	89
4877	257	5647	235	6528	202	7536	154	8687	88
4633	244	5421	226	6333	196	7386	151	8601	87
4401	232	5204	217	6143	190	7238	148	8515	86
4181	220	4996	208	5958	184	7093	145	8429	85
3972	209	4796	200	5780	179	6951	142	8345	84
3774	199	4604	192	5606	173	6812	139	8262	83
3585	189	4420	184	5438	168	6676	136	8179	83
3585	–	4420	–	5438	–	6676	–	8179	–

As can be seen from table 4.1, several things occur when fixed fractional position sizing is used. Firstly, the ending balances after 20 consecutive losing trades differ considerably depending on how much is risked on each trade. While the opposite is also true, my concern here is one of risk management and creating longevity and this should not be confused with trading for maximum profit. The next factor is that the actual dollar amount risked per trade decreases and will continue to do so to the point that it becomes so small you may not be able to place a trade.

Natural compounding will also occur, as shown in table 4.2. Here the results are shown for 20 consecutive winners with varying risk percentages. For the purposes of the table, I have assumed that only as much as was risked was won in each trade. Of course, in reality, profits for a winning trade are potentially limitless.

Table 4.2: varying account balances after 20 consecutive winners

Balance	5%	Balance	4%	Balance	3%	Balance	2%	Balance	1%
10000		10000		10000		10000		10000	
10500	500	10400	400	10300	300	10200	200	10100	100
11025	525	10816	416	10609	309	10404	204	10201	101
11576	551	11249	433	10927	318	10612	208	10303	102
12155	579	11699	450	11255	328	10824	212	10406	103
12763	608	12167	468	11593	338	11041	216	10510	104
13401	638	12653	487	11941	348	11262	221	10615	105
14071	670	13159	506	12299	358	11487	225	10721	106
14775	704	13686	526	12668	369	11717	230	10829	107
15513	739	14233	547	13048	380	11951	234	10937	108
16289	776	14802	569	13439	391	12190	239	11046	109
17103	814	15395	592	13842	403	12434	244	11157	110
17959	855	16010	616	14258	415	12682	249	11268	112
18856	898	16651	640	14685	428	12936	254	11381	113
19799	943	17317	666	15126	441	13195	259	11495	114
20789	990	18009	693	15580	454	13459	264	11610	115
21829	1039	18730	720	16047	467	13728	269	11726	116
22920	1091	19479	749	16528	481	14002	275	11843	117
24066	1146	20258	779	17024	496	14282	280	11961	118
25270	1203	21068	810	17535	511	14568	286	12081	120
26533	1263	21911	843	18061	526	14859	291	12202	121
26533		21911		18061		14859		12202	

Clearly, there are two sides to the risk equation but the following three cornerstone rules must be considered:

1 If you lose all your capital, you will not be able to trade.

2 The more you lose, the harder is becomes mentally to continue to trade.

3 The only thing you can control is how much you lose.

Table 4.3 shows how many consecutive trades it will take to lose 50 per cent of the account balance, which seems to be a common benchmark for new traders, based on percentage risked per trade.

Table 4.3: number of losing trades before a 50 per cent equity decline

Risk per trade	No. of trades for a 50% equity decline
1%	69
2%	35
3%	23
4%	17
5%	14

Each person will have a different risk profile, so it's now just a balancing act to find your own risk/reward point and stick to that as part of your trading plan. I use 2 per cent risk per trade as a guide but a private trader could go to around 3 per cent. As a rule of thumb, if you start to move toward 5 per cent, you're looking for trouble and possibly being too aggressive with the risk.

Risk management using leverage

In the past, the use of leverage has been confined to exchange traded options (ETOs), warrants or futures contracts. Today, however, the popularity of CFDs has exploded, and they will continue to transform the trading possibilities on the ASX in the same way as they already have in the US and Europe. In the UK, 30 per cent of trading volumes are traded via CFDs. In Australia, we have mainly seen second- or third-tier firms offering the product; however, at the time of writing, two top-tier firms have entered the fray and more should soon follow as the popularity of CFDs and people's understanding of them grow.

CFDs are highly leveraged products and as such need to be traded and managed with a different line of thinking than what most people are used to when trading normal shares. With normal shares, the amount that may be lost is usually very restricted to the capital outlaid. With CFDs, though, the capital outlay required is minimal in comparison to the total value of the investment. This tends to make people think they should use all the capital available to them, just like when they trade normal shares. This is plain wrong and can be fraught with danger.

Let's highlight this point using a simple example that shows how leverage actually works. Say you have $20 000 to trade with and you feel that the price Brambles is trading at has some potential to move higher. You wish to buy at $8.85 and place a protective stop at $8.50, or a risk of $0.35. In terms of your account, you do not wish to lose more than $500, so you can buy 1428 shares (500 ÷ 0.35), which will mean an outlay of $12 637 (1428 × $8.85). The problem is that $12 637 represents over 63 per cent of your available funds and investing this amount will mean you won't be able to take any more trades until this one has been completed. This can be construed as being 'riskier' than using leverage. It doesn't allow diversification, a prime ingredient in successful trading, especially during strong trending markets.

With CFDs, however, we only need to place a small amount of that $12 637 with the broker — indeed, the amount required may be as small as 5 per cent to 10 per cent, depending on your provider. If it is 5 per cent, we need only place $632 ($12 637 × 0.05) toward the trade, yet are still able to purchase the 1428 shares we need. If the trade is a loss, we will still lose $500 of the $20 000 but we only needed to use $632 to do it, rather than $12 637. Therefore, we have a lot more money available to us to take other trades and better apply our trading skills and reduce our risk through diversification.

However, it's this last point that can get people into trouble with leverage. Because they have only outlaid $632, many people turn the equation inside out and do one of two things. Firstly, they may say that their account balance is really $400 000 ($20 000 ÷ 0.05) because that's how much they can control with the leverage. Secondly, they may buy $400 000 worth of shares with their $20 000. When using leverage you should not concern yourself with the underlying value of the stock you can control. After trading futures for the last 20 years, I can comfortably say that I have never known how much the underlying commodity I held was worth. Why? Apart from the fact that it is not relevant to you as a trader, it puts you on the wrong line of thinking regarding risk.

The only relevant point is how much your loss will be if you get stopped out and what percentage of your account balance it represents. This is the key. In other words, I work backwards from the risk to the underlying value, not the reverse. I calculate the entry point, then the protective stop point. That is my risk. In the Brambles example above, it was $0.35. Then I divide that into the account risk — in my example, $500. Then, and only then, will I know how many shares I will buy and, as a consequence of all these factors, what outlay will be required. The risk is always the determinant of the amount of shares purchased and therefore the dollars outlaid. If you can start to think along these lines, you will be better placed to protect yourself from an extreme event that may destroy your capital and land you in some serious financial trouble.

Level of diversification

There is one more element to consider — how many positions to have on. Again, using a risk management tool we can correctly define this, rather than having to take a wild guess according to our confidence levels. When the stock market is moving along strongly, as it was from 2003 to 2005, the inclination is to get onto anything that moves. Because of the leverage available from CFDs, this can be a very dangerous proposition and one that must be controlled. The question is how many positions should you take? Five? Eight? More?

The answer lies in the amount of margin being used. In the previous example with Brambles, we put up $632 in margin to cover the position. The $632 represented 3.16 per cent of our $20 000 account. This percentage is known as the margin to equity ratio and, ideally, it should not exceed 30 per cent to 35 per cent to remain on the safe side. As prices move around and your protective stops are adjusted, this ratio will also move, so you should keep monitoring it in case it starts to creep beyond the 35 per cent level. If it starts to get toward 50 per cent, the exposure to the market should a nasty price reversal occur is starting to become dangerous.

Some CFD providers offer a guaranteed stop loss (GSL) facility that enables the margin to be lowered even further and again helps you reduce your risk. The GSL facility is a great idea when you are going against the major trend or shorting a very low-priced stock that may be a takeover target.

Capital restrictions with non-leveraged trading

Before the days of CFDs, when the market was extremely bullish on the coat-tails of the US technology boom in the late 1990s, I came across the problem of having too many trading signals and not enough capital to trade them all. I needed some type of filter that allowed me to make an educated guess as to which of two stocks might be a better performer should they both be winners. I named the filter 'Bang for Buck' and it eventually found its way into the Metastock user guide as well as several trading books. (The coding required to program the Bang for Buck filter into various trading software is provided in appendix C.)

Stock selection without leverage has one serious drawback — it means buying $10 000 of BHP is very different to buying $10 000 of a sub-$10 stock, as capital usage in higher priced stocks is inefficient compared with lower priced stocks. A good exercise to prove this is to compare the average price range of a stock over the last 200 days with its current price.

For example, BHP has a 200-day average price range of $0.32 with a current underlying price of approximately $21.00. Using $10 000, you could buy 476 shares with an expected profit of $152 per day (0.32 × 476). Compare this to EPT, which has a 200-day average price range of $0.035 with a current underlying price of $0.44. This enables us to buy 22 727 shares with the $10 000. Here the expected daily profit would be $795 (0.035 × 22 727). In this example, we'd get more 'bang for our buck' by buying EPT and not BHP. So if I received a buy signal in EPT and one in BHP, in theory I should be better off taking the EPT trade and forgoing the BHP.

The Bang for Buck simply filters the relative volatility of the stock in comparison to its price. As I pointed out above, buying $10 000 worth of BHP is very different to buying $10 000 worth of EPT. While you may get the BHP trade correct, based on the capital used the results will not be overly efficient. We need to get our money's worth and we need to make profits with the least amount of work. Over the long term, concentrating on the EPT-type trades is more efficient.

To calculate the Bang for Buck filter, simply divide the amount in your trading account (say, $10 000) by the closing price of the stock on any given day. This number is then multiplied by the average range of the stock for the last 200 days. (The average range is the average distance the stock has moved from its high to low point each day over the last 200 days.) Divide this number by 100 to convert the result to dollars and cents, which in turn indicates the possible dollar return on any given day. The higher the expected profit versus required investment, the higher the profit potential, meaning selecting higher ratios will enable stock selection with potential for movement and this is what we want.

PART II

MAPPING
THE MARKET

CHAPTER 5
STEP ONE — DEFINING THE TREND

I believe the correct study of the markets — and therefore technical analysis — is about understanding what price action is important and what is not. With over 1700 stocks listed on the ASX, it is imperative to be able to quickly recognise price action that may result in a profitable situation. I can scan 300 price charts within a few hours, but I can only do so because I intuitively know what I'm looking for.

I take a three-step approach in the trading process — step one, and the cornerstone of my analysis, is to understand where the particular share price is with regard to its current trend; step two is to find further evidence of important levels where change may take place; lastly, step three is to be on the alert for the low-risk set-ups that will present themselves at various intervals within the trend. In essence, this is my trading plan, albeit without the risk management. It's how I've always traded and it's what I'm comfortable doing.

Defining trends using moving averages

The trend of a market can be defined in various ways. The simplest way, and one that I suggest new traders should investigate as a starting point, is moving averages. Through using a simple moving average, you can identify the trend of various time frames. The shorter term trend can be defined using a 20-day moving average, for example, whereas the longer term trend can be defined with a longer dated moving average — say, 80 days or more — as shown in figure 5.1. The application of moving averages can be used on any time frame.

Figure 5.1: various trends defined by moving averages

After a period of watching price action and the relationship between it and moving averages, you can start to see limitations. One limitation is that a moving average as an indicator lags price action and will therefore be quite slow in notifying you of a change in trend. This is especially true when a market turns very sharply, such as what occurred in PaperlinX Ltd (PPX) in June 2005. The absolute low of the downtrend occurred on 1 June; however, the moving average didn't really start moving higher until 21 June. By then, prices had already climbed 30 per cent. This is shown in figure 5.2.

Another limitation of moving averages is that they cannot really help a great deal in determining the depth of a retracement that may simply be a part of an ongoing trend. Retracements within trends offer extremely profitable low-risk opportunities for those willing to exploit shorter term moves. However, to do so requires rigid rules that really cannot be applied and tested within a simplistic approach that only uses moving averages.

Figure 5.2: the typical lag of moving averages behind price action

Another shortcoming of a moving average is that markets can exhibit sustained periods of sideways price action. During such times, a moving average is all but useless as a guide and is best left aside until the trend resumes.

A more robust determinant of a trend than moving averages is the ebb and flow of price action itself.

Market swings

All markets gyrate, or swing, back and forth. Sometimes these swings are very long and sustained; at other times, they are small and choppy. Almost all of the time, larger swings are made up of smaller swings, which in turn are made of even smaller swings. As such, all price action is known as fractal. A fractal is 'a geometric pattern that is repeated at even smaller scales to produce irregular shapes'.[1] There are two ways we can view these swings. Regardless of whether we are looking at a monthly chart, then looking at the same period on a weekly, a daily or even on a 60-minute chart (or even further), swings of various

---

1   Source: <www.dictionary.com>.

sizes can be observed. Observing the same price action across various charts is usually referred to as using multiple time frames.

The second method is to observe one time frame — say, a daily chart — then watch for swings that travel certain distances in relation to others on the same chart and time frame. These swings are measured in degrees, where the smallest degree is the smallest swing and the largest degree is the largest swing. Figure 5.3 shows a daily chart of Bank of Queensland Ltd (BOQ). Can you identify the swings?

Figure 5.3: Typical price action

In figure 5.3, various swings can be seen, some large and some small. However, it is important to relate these swings to each other in terms of their size (or their degree). The swings can be compared using various different measurements — for example, they can be measured as a percentage move of the underlying price, or by the number of dollars and cents the price has travelled.

Figure 5.4 shows the same BOQ chart as figure 5.3, except I told the computer to show the swings that were greater than 20 per cent of the underlying price. You can see five swings in figure 5.4 — three swings up that are punctuated by two smaller swings down. All the swings relate to each other because their lengths in either direction exceed by 20 per cent price movement in the opposite direction.

Figure 5.4: BOQ with 20 per cent price swings highlighted

To visually illustrate the fractal pattern, let's take the same chart of BOQ but use 10 per cent swings instead of 20 per cent, as shown in figure 5.5. Now you can see smaller swings, which represent smaller trends within the larger trends outlined in figure 5.4. Again, they are all related because they are of the same degree. Therefore, these 10 per cent swings sit within the 20 per cent swings.

Figure 5.5: BOQ with 10 per cent price swings highlighted

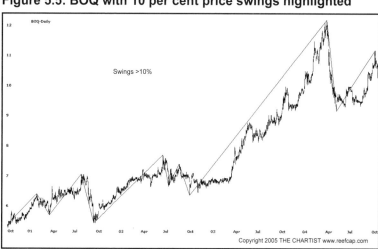

Taking this one step further, we can tell the computer to identify 5 per cent swings, as shown in figure 5.6. This chart shows even smaller trends within the intermediate trends, which in turn lie within the larger trends — that is, 5 per cent swings sit within 10 per cent swings that sit within 20 per cent swings.

Figure 5.6: BOQ with 5 per cent price swings highlighted

As we drill down into the chart with each lower degree swing, we get more 'noise'. (Noise includes price fluctuations that can confuse chart interpretation and therefore market direction.) A noisy chart is one that should be either avoided or clarified by arranging the swings into patterns. If we can successfully interpret these patterns and place them in order, we are in the very strong position of being better able to identify the next move. The most advanced way of doing this is by applying the Elliott wave principle.

Defining trends using Elliott wave

If you have heard of Elliott wave (EW) theory and dismissed it, I urge you to read the following interpretation before skipping to a later part of the book. EW has received a mixed reception over the years and it does not surprise me that sceptics abound. Either you love it or hate it. I won't suggest that those who hate it don't understand it, but I will suggest that they should perhaps look at it from a very different perspective to what has already been offered by hard-core enthusiasts.

First, let me say that I only use EW to define the trend. I do not use it as a stand-alone trading device. One of the main reasons why EW has been misconstrued is because there are notable analysts who attempt to use it to account for all price action going back many, many years. Unless you are an analyst first and foremost, I think this is the wrong route to take. As a trader — not an analyst — I believe EW can offer an exceptional insight into the swings that occur within share prices.

If you are a hard-nosed EW analyst, you might think that this limited use would lead to an inaccurate interpretation of the bigger picture. However, through forcing patterns onto price action and in turn adding too much subjectivity to a simple rule-based method, many EW analysts get their analysis wrong. As an example, a purist may attempt to analyse the chart of Mayne Group (MAY) shown in figure 5.7 — which to me shows no discernible patterns — in a way that is a recipe for disaster.

Figure 5.7: Mayne price action with no discernible patterns

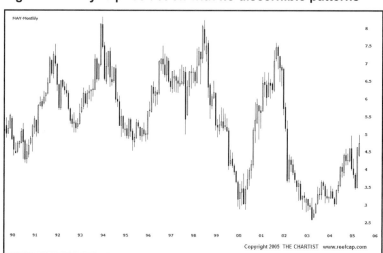

My view, rightly or wrongly, is that patterns must be easily recognisable and defined — they must hit you between the eyes before the theory can be applied. If the patterns don't stand out, chances are they don't exist and you're attempting to force the theory to fit somewhere it may not apply.

Some argue that EW theory is applicable on just 50 per cent of occasions. I'm not sure how that fits in relation to the ASX, but I can certainly find plenty of instances where no patterns are recognisable. In that situation, as in the MAY example above, I stand aside. As there are 1700 stocks to choose from, we can afford to be very selective and ensure we only review those stock prices that show blatantly obvious patterns.

To me, EW is the world's most advanced trend identifier. As will become even clearer through the remainder of this chapter, unlike many purists, I do not use EW as a stand-alone tool. I apply it for trend purposes first then utilise low-risk patterns if and when they appear according to the directives offered by EW.

Elliott wave theory — the basics

This section will not provide an in-depth analysis of the complexities of EW — a lot has already been written on the topic and most is freely available on the internet.

However, I will discuss the basics briefly. Ralph Nelson Elliott developed the wave principle in the late 1920s. He found that stock markets traded in repetitive cycles and patterns that were very closely aligned to Dow theory. Elliott suggested markets operate in a series of trends and corrections that formed waves — outlined as swings earlier with our Bank of Queensland examples. He called the trends 'impulsive waves' and the moves against the trend 'corrective waves'. Elliott went further to suggest that impulsive waves usually occurred in sets of three and were punctuated by two corrective waves, making the pattern a total of five waves. From there he noted that after five waves in one direction, which he labelled with the numerals one through five, prices would decline in a three-wave pattern, which he labelled with the letters a, b, c. According to Elliott, a completed bullish pattern looks like the pattern shown in figure 5.8.

Figure 5.8: Elliott's theoretical formation of waves

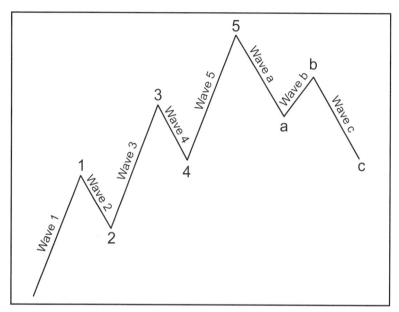

A completed bearish pattern is simply the inverse to the pattern shown in figure 5.8.

This completed structure is part of a fractal — that is, it is either made up of smaller and similar patterns or it is part of a larger pattern. Let's take a look at an example, this time using a monthly chart of Bank of Queensland, shown in figure 5.9. On the chart you can clearly see five waves up, three of which are impulsive (labelled 1, 3 and 5) and two corrective (labelled 2 and 4), followed by a three-wave decline (labelled A, B and C).

The first thing to understand is that real-world examples are not as clean as the theoretical examples you'll find in textbooks; however, you can see the basic shape. Soon I'll add very specific rules that will help clarify the patterns even more. For now, though, you can clearly see the swings.

Figure 5.9: BOQ example of the completed wave pattern

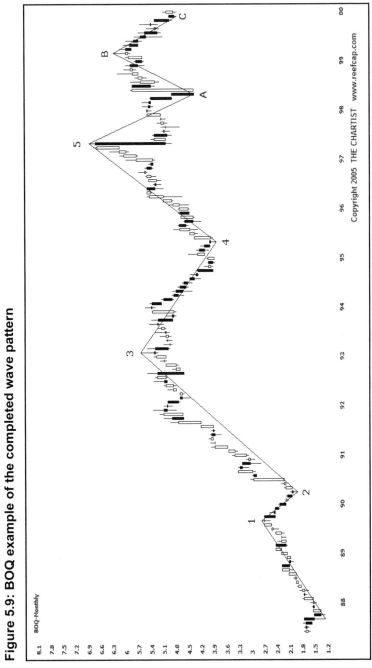

Because this is a fractal, the completed pattern must contain smaller patterns within it, or be a part of a larger pattern. If we assume that it sits within a larger pattern, the high, or the peak of the fifth wave, must be the completion of a larger first wave and the low, marked as wave C, will be the completion of a larger second wave. Because we're now discussing a pattern with swings of a larger degree (remember our 20 per cent and 10 per cent swing charts), we need to label it slightly differently so we know which pattern is being referred to. I will label the larger pattern, shown in figure 5.10, as wave (1) through wave (5). What we now have is a larger wave (1) that is made up of the five smaller waves shown in figure 5.9, and the wave (2) decline that is made up of the A, B, C waves from the smaller pattern. This is a fractal at work.

If this interpretation is correct, we should be able to see the fractal continue to grow and continue the pattern — in other words, wave (3) should be the next movement seen in the chart. Remember that wave (3) is an impulsive wave that should continue in the same direction as wave (1). The pattern at the time of writing (June 2005) is shown in figure 5.11.

Figure 5.11 shows the next swing higher, which is wave (3), is occurring — also note that it again contains a smaller five-wave structure of which we've just completed wave one through wave four. If this is to continue according to the wave principle, when the smaller fifth wave completes we will have also completed the larger wave (3). What should occur after the larger wave (3) has completed? Wave (4), a decline, should follow and in turn this should be followed by the last wave in the pattern, a wave (5).

Figure 5.12 shows a weekly chart of Newcrest Mining Ltd (NCM). In the chart, larger swings subdivide into smaller swings and those in turn subdivide into even smaller swings. This is a classic fractal. When we start to see these waves develop, we can then apply rules to guide us toward trading opportunities.

Figure 5.10: the fractal at work — the smaller pattern within the larger pattern

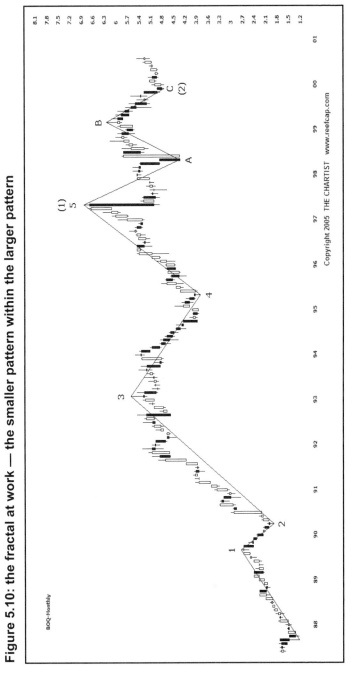

Figure 5.11: the fractal continues to grow

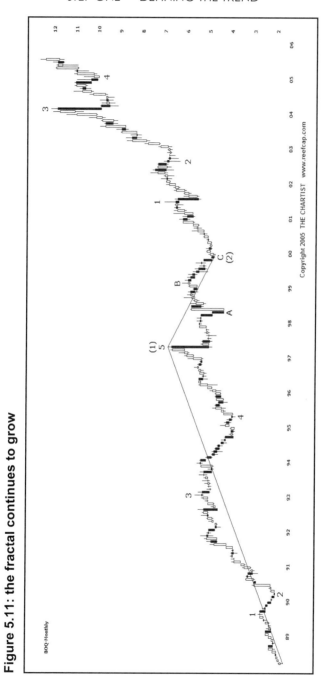

BOQ-Monthly

Copyright 2005 THE CHARTIST   www.reefcap.com

Figure 5.12: NCM showing subdivisions of waves

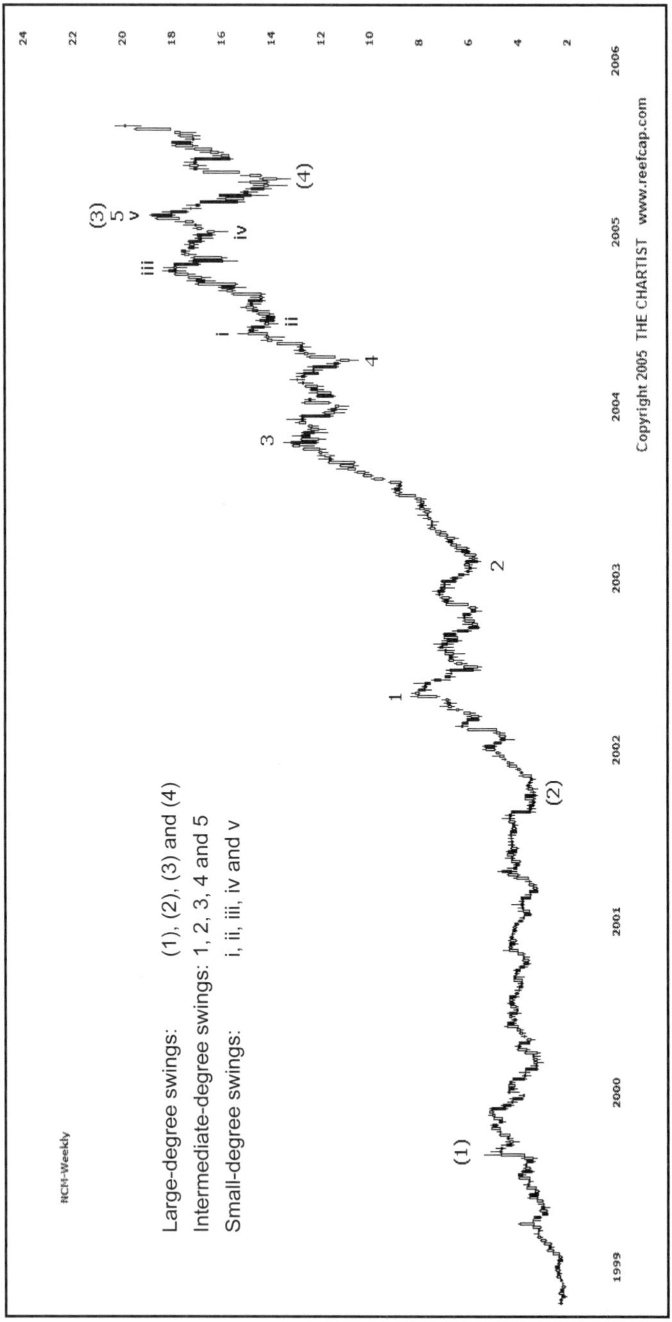
NCM-Weekly
Large-degree swings: (1), (2), (3) and (4)
Intermediate-degree swings: 1, 2, 3, 4 and 5
Small-degree swings: i, ii, iii, iv and v
(1)
(2)
1
2
3
4
i
ii
iii
iv
(3)
5
v
(4)
24
22
20
18
16
14
12
10
8
6
4
2
1999
2000
2001
2002
2003
2004
2005
2006
Copyright 2005 THE CHARTIST www.reefcap.com

In summary, a set of waves makes up a repeating pattern that will tend to subdivide on numerous occasions into similar patterns with the same basic characteristics. This is the repeating fractal pattern known as the Elliott wave principle — arguably the most advanced trend analysis tool available.

Elliott wave theory as a forecasting tool

Another misunderstood or misinterpreted part of EW is that it is a forecasting tool. While this may appear to be its purpose on the surface, I believe this assumption is incorrect and I certainly don't use it in that context. EW sets parameters for three specific rules that must be continually proven for the theory to remain in place. If any of the rules are breached, the analysis, or count as it's known, is wrong.

Along with the strict rules there are several guidelines, which is where most of the conjecture surrounding EW arises. Guidelines are considered common traits of EW price action that tend to occur more often than not. Like the rules, these guidelines build an equation that proves or disproves analysis and so can sound warning bells rather than give blatant right or wrong signals. For the most part, the conjecture or criticism arises because the list of guidelines put forth by experts seems to grow — especially, it seems, when the analyst requires yet another one to justify his or her current analysis. I overcome this by limiting the scope of the analysis to the core rules, some basic guidelines and some associated classical charting patterns.

Because of its ability to prove or disprove itself, EW becomes invaluable in highlighting exactly where your analysis will be wrong and so where you should exit the position. These levels can be clearly identified before a position is initiated. Hence, combined with low-risk entries, EW is a powerful tool — but one that works best when kept simple and when the analyst is a trader first and foremost.

Elliott wave theory — the rules

Firstly, let's look at the unbreakable rules. If you attempt EW analysis, you *must* adhere to these simple rules to the letter. They are non-negotiable. The rules are:

1 Wave two can never retrace below the start of wave one.

2 Wave three is usually the longest, but can never be the shortest.

3 Wave four can never retrace to overlap the top of wave one.

Let's take a look at an example. Figure 5.13 shows the price action for Smorgon Steel Group Ltd (SSX), in which I initiated a position for clients at $1.00 in April 2004. I was able to ride the trend and exit at $1.38 about 12 months later, meaning not only was I able to gain 38 per cent in growth, but I also collected the dividends along the way.

Figure 5.13: price action for SSX

As can be seen in figure 5.13, after the first peak at $1.11, prices retraced back to $0.96. I read this as wave one to $1.11 and then a possible wave-two decline to $0.96. If prices had declined below $0.90, the start of wave one, my analysis would clearly be wrong according to the rules of EW. Therefore, my protective stop should be placed just below $0.90. Prices started to rise from the low at $0.96 and the first rule, which states that wave two must not decline below the start of wave one, had been satisfied.

At this stage, no-one can know what prices will do — we're still requiring the rules to be proven as prices unfold. Rule two states that wave three is usually the longest but can never be the shortest. I knew that wave one was $0.21 in length ($1.11 – $0.90), so for rule two to be proven correct, wave three must be a minimum of $0.21 in length and therefore exceed $1.17 ($0.96 + $0.21). Prices continued past this point to $1.28. After prices hit $1.28, a decline to $1.15 was seen. The depth of this decline suggested that wave three had ended. Because wave two was $0.32 in length, it exceeded the minimum distance required, meaning the EW principle was continuing to prove itself.

The last rule states that wave four cannot end below the end of wave one. We know the first wave ended at $1.11, so if this level is breached, the analysis will have been disproved. It therefore becomes logical to raise the protective stop to just below $1.11. Prices did dip to $1.15 before turning around. It is impossible to know beforehand whether prices would stop here, but I did know that if the market went through $1.11, the analysis is incorrect and the position should be exited immediately. This also becomes a point to pyramid or add to the position because you know exactly where you'll be wrong and can place an appropriate protective stop.

The reason I exited at $1.38 will be explained shortly, but for now we have a definite EW pattern because the three core rules were all proven.

This is a very straightforward example of the rules continuing to prove themselves as prices unfold. You must be aware at what points the rules will show themselves to fail and so know where to exit and reassess the analysis.

Figure 5.14 shows an example of the rules failing to prove themselves. The chart shows the price movement of ResMed Inc (RMD). As you can clearly see, rules one and two were satisfied — wave two did not decline below the start of wave one and wave three is longer than wave one. The problem came when prices over the last two days shown on the chart dropped below the high made by wave one. The principle was disproved because rule three had been broken. At this point, the position should be exited immediately. Remember — EW must continually prove itself.

Figure 5.14: rule three failed to be proven

Because the five-wave structure is a fractal, we should be alert to a smaller degree pattern showing signs of failure. If a smaller degree pattern does fail, there is a chance that the larger pattern is also starting to fail. Figure 5.15 shows my current interpretation of ANZ. The larger degree waves suggest that the fourth wave has been completed and prices are now tracing out the last or fifth wave. Notice that this fifth wave appears to be subdividing into a smaller structure that is currently in a wave iii. If this is to remain intact according to our rules, the high of wave i should not be broken by a wave-iv decline. I have therefore noted in my charts to be aware that if this level is broken, perhaps the larger pattern is also starting to fail. If this is extrapolated out to the larger wave pattern, prices need to remain above the high of wave one or the trade should be exited.

Figure 5.15: smaller degree patterns within a larger degree pattern

The reason for becoming bearish on the above stock is because the larger five-wave pattern would have been completed and we know that this should be followed by a three-wave corrective pattern. Figure 5.16 shows such an example — when the price action of Sally Malay Mining Ltd (SMY) completed five waves up, it was followed by a three-wave decline. But note the decline represented a 50 per cent drop in its share price in just a matter of months. Even a die-hard, long-term investor will start to quiver when prices decline by that amount. However, as part of the larger degree pattern, wave (4) has still not declined past the peak of wave (1), so EW has not yet been disproved, and the fifth, impulsive, wave in the larger degree pattern should follow.

Elliott wave theory — the guidelines

Guidelines are attributes that are familiar parts within EW — that is, they are usually seen but not required like the rules. Guidelines are exactly that — guides to what is usually expected. The list of guidelines can be long and, unfortunately, it has grown over the years; however, I find that, used with simple interpretation, they can be well worth keeping an eye on.

Figure 5.16: using an understanding of what is expected to highlight potential loss scenarios

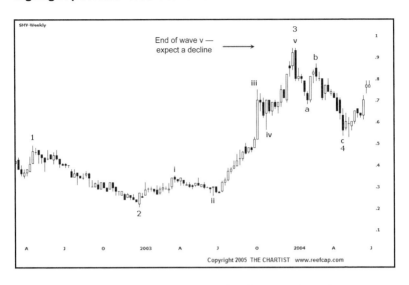

Guideline one: impulsive waves tend to be smooth and strong; corrective waves tend to be choppy and messy

One of the easiest ways to start seeing waves is to first identify any choppy or messy price action. This tends to indicate corrective wave structures and will therefore often be preceded and followed by an impulsive wave. Conversely, smooth, free-running price action tends to indicate the trends or impulsive waves.

Figure 5.17 shows a weekly chart of Billabong (BBG), which listed in late 2000. Added to the chart is the percentage swing indicator. There is clear evidence of smooth trends from the moment the stock listed, followed by choppy price action on the first major decline of magnitude and length. Because prices didn't decline past the low point at listing (rule one) and that the decline was very messy, this becomes a very simple wave-two pattern to recognise. You can see the clear benefits of recognising such a pattern, because it is highly likely that a wave two will be followed by a powerful impulsive third wave. In this example, prices increased by 300 per cent over the next two years.

Figure 5.17: impulsive waves versus corrective waves

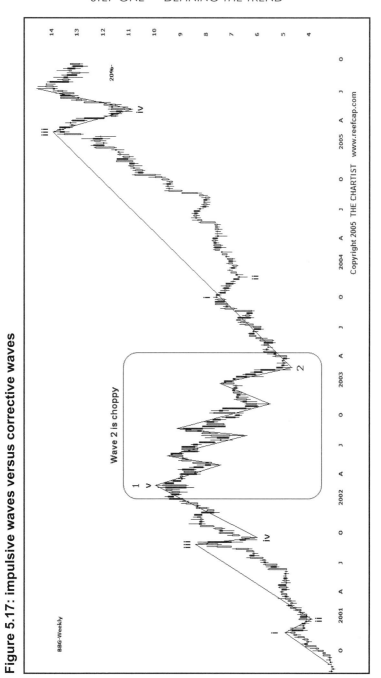

Guideline two: wave two tends to retrace between 50 per cent and 70 per cent of wave one

Guideline two is your first measuring tool, and it can alert you to the fact that an EW pattern may be forming. Wave two tends to be a deeper correction than wave four. This is often because market participants aren't convinced of the initial upside momentum that was offered in wave one. Wave two should not retrace past the start of wave one, but more often than not it will retrace at least 50 per cent to 70 per cent of the length of the first wave.

Figure 5.18, depicting the price action of ANZ, shows two separate examples of this guideline. The larger wave two that ended in late May declined to a point just past the 50 per cent point of wave one. The smaller wave ii, ending in August, also declined past the 50 per cent point of the smaller wave i.

Guideline three: wave four tends to retrace between 30 per cent to 50 per cent of wave three

After wave three has commenced, the market usually realises that the trend is strong. As a result, any declines in the latter parts of the trend tend to be shorter than those in the earlier parts. This is why wave four tends to be shorter than wave two — people are quick to enter on the dip. Wave four also tends to create more of a sideways or triangular pattern and is a precursor to a quick breakout to new highs.

The price action of AMP Ltd, shown in figure 5.19, is a good example of a typical pattern. Wave two was deeper because at that stage investors were not convinced that a turnaround was imminent. However, at wave four, after a very strong third wave, investors were a lot happier to buy in at the dip. Because of this, the dip was smaller — in this case, not even quite making it to 30 per cent. Notice also that wave four is triangular in shape.

Figure 5.18: wave two retracement as 50 per cent to 70 per cent of wave one

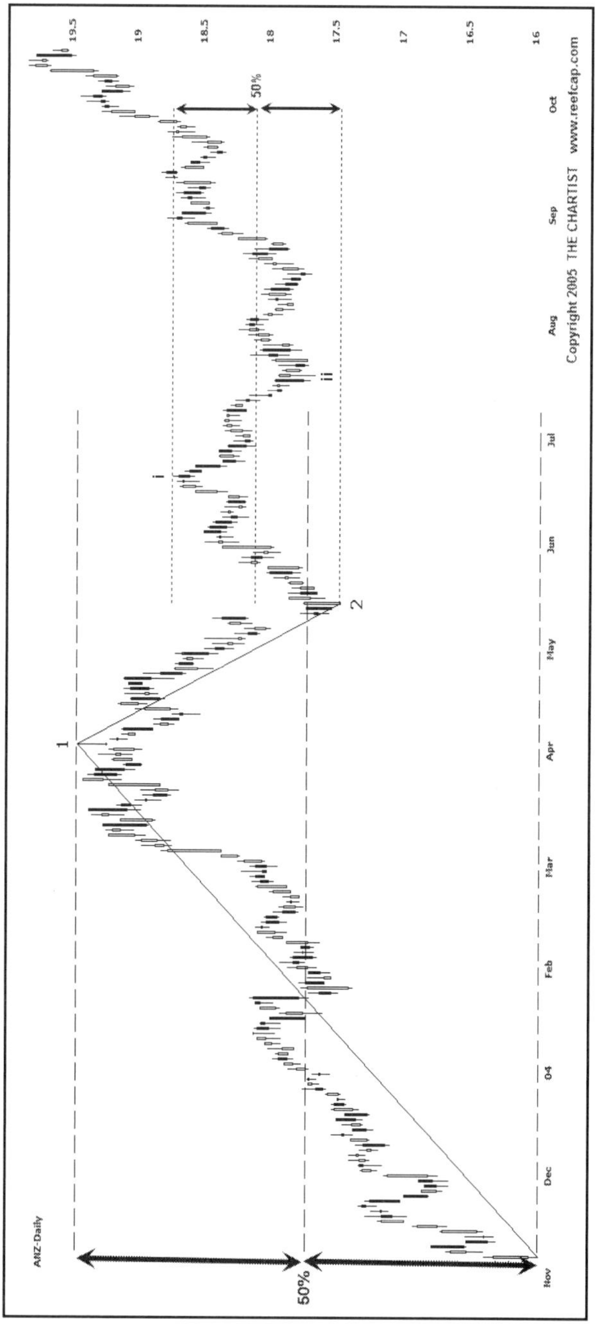

Figure 5.19: wave two versus wave four

Guideline 4: wave one and wave five tend to be the same length

Earlier I discussed a weekly trade in SSX where I had taken profits at $1.38. This guideline was the reason for that action. Once the length of wave five equals that of wave one, I start to tighten the stop and look for warning signs of a reversal. This is a critical area because the trend has now aged and only latecomers are joining the fray at these higher levels. Remember that after wave five is completed, we get a large sell off — which occurred here.

Figure 5.20 shows the level at which the fifth wave in the SSX pattern equalled the length of the first wave. As can be seen, prices just popped a little higher than the $1.38 level. This extra pop was caused in part by a lot of analysts upgrading their forecasts and several newsletter services placing buy recommendations on the stock. Under the right circumstances, this became a great contrarian trade for EW traders.

Figure 5.20: wave five versus wave one

Guideline five: corrective wave A and corrective wave C tend to be the same length

In the earlier theoretical diagram of the wave principle shown in figure 5.8, it was noted that after there is a five-wave advance, there is a three-wave corrective move. These three corrective waves are labelled A, B and C, but they also occur as part of waves two and four. As you may be starting to see, there is a lot of proportion involved in the waves and patterns, and this guideline continues that theme. I am always on the lookout for the start of an impulsive wave when wave C gets to the same distance as wave A during a corrective move. Figure 5.21 shows the price action that occurred after wave C reached the same length as wave A on the CBA chart.

Figure 5.21: wave A versus wave C

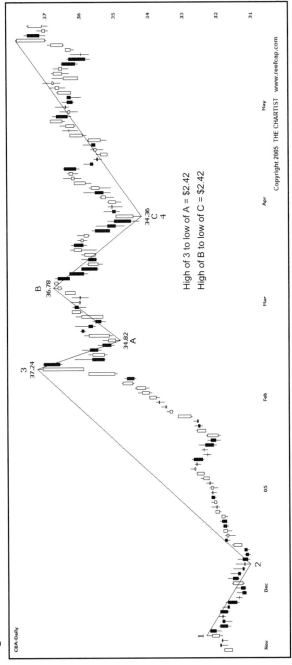

CBA-Daily

High of 3 to low of A = $2.42
High of B to low of C = $2.42

Copyright 2005 THE CHARTIST www.reefcap.com

Figure 5.21 shows the daily price action of CBA where the market corrects in a perfect A-B-C pattern to complete wave four. Wave C matches the distance of wave A at $34.36 and then runs over the distance by just a few cents. This was however the low day before the larger fifth wave commenced its ascent to new highs.

Many guidelines exist, but the above five are the ones I find to be the most valuable. Remember that it's important not to get too tied up in the deep analytics of it all as, believe me, there are plenty more. I recently read the rules and guidelines a charting program was based on that went for eleven pages. Will that amount of depth *really* increase your bottom line? Stay with the trader mentality and stay away from being a perfectionist-analyst.

As mentioned, one aspect that you will pick up from these guidelines is the concept of *proportion*. The best EW patterns tend to be very nicely proportioned, so when you come across one that is not well-proportioned, a closer inspection is warranted to ensure that a secondary pattern is not forming that misleads your initial lines of thinking.

The following weekly charts of ASX Ltd, Macquarie Ltd (MBL), Seven Network Ltd (SEV) and Pacific Brands Ltd (PBG) — figures 5.22 to 5.25 — all show even proportions, which suggests the current counts are accurate at this stage.

Conversely, the chart of Babcock & Brown Ltd (BNB) shown in figure 5.26 is an example where the corrective fourth wave is not particularly well-proportioned compared to the prior corrective second wave. This may mean that either the count is incorrect or that the second impulsive leg is part of a different degree wave and may need to be re-labelled at some stage in the future.

Figure 5.22: a well-proportioned ASX trend

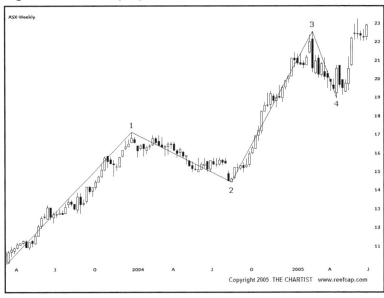

Figure 5.23: a well-proportioned MBL trend

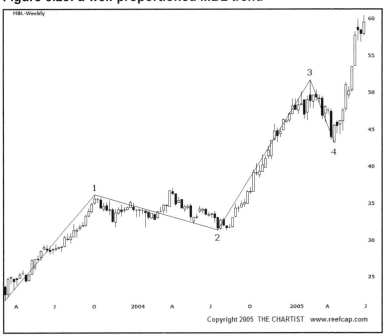

Figure 5.24: a well-proportioned SEV trend

Figure 5.25: a well-proportioned PBG bearish trend

Figure 5.26: out of proportion wave four versus wave two

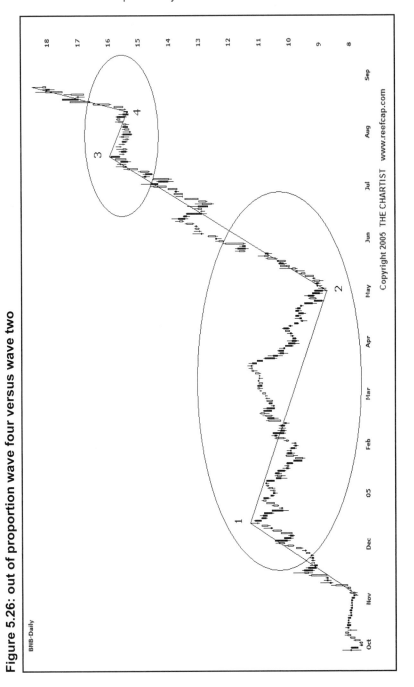

BNB-Daily

The chart of Australian Worldwide Exploration (AWE) shown in figure 5.27 abides by all the EW rules; however, the last leg, or wave five, is somewhat out of proportion or stretched in comparison to wave one. Only time will tell if the current labelling will indeed be correct.

Figure 5.27: wave v out of proportion to wave i

CHAPTER 6

WHERE TO LOOK FOR NEW PATTERNS

Hard-nosed theorists will start their counting back from the start of historical prices. To analyse the Dow Jones over the last 200 years in order to ascertain current price action may be the proper way for the pure theorist, but to me, with my trader mentality, price swings that may take the next 25 years to fulfil are just not interesting. I'm simply concerned with possible patterns that fit with my time frame of trading. If I were a day trader looking at a five-minute chart, I probably wouldn't have a great deal of interest in the monthly wave count. In my style of trading I use daily charts, so I may refer to weekly charts to see the 'lie of the land', but rarely will I use a monthly chart.

In some of the examples shown in chapter 5, we had an obvious starting point for the EW structures — the day the stock listed. It has also been suggested that wave counts can be started from major highs and lows. I agree that for shares with a long price history, this is better than looking at prices from the start of time, and is one direction that I automatically moved toward. As an extension of this, I also look at intermediate highs and lows, especially after a breakout into new territory or through a major trend line. These trend lines can either be horizontal or diagonal, with the greater the importance of the trend line, the more notice you should take. (A trend line gains more importance the more often it is touched by prices. If it is touched two or three times, it is considered reasonably strong; however, if it is touched five or more times, it is considered extremely strong.) When a trend line gets broken, prices will usually come back to it before moving off again. This is the typical ebb and flow of prices and is how EW patterns come about. Also be on the alert when you see a double bottom or top, or points where a substantial low or high is retested, because five-wave patterns can start from any of these points.

The weekly chart of CBA in figure 6.1 shows the share's all-time high was followed by a major low. The fact that the all-time high (an important resistance line) was breached suggests the trend was definitely up, but there were no indications of a possible wave count. Remember — if the pattern doesn't stand out and hit you between the eyes, it's probably not there. A purist may be able to discern this price action, but I don't have the time or the trader's inclination to force something onto the picture.

Figure 6.1: undefined price action

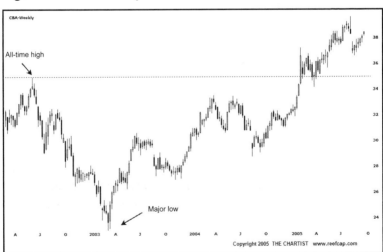

Figure 6.2 (on page 90) shows a segment of the weekly chart from figure 6.1, but on a daily level. Until the all-time high was breached, there was no specific count available. However, once that high was

broken we were able to start to see a promising three-wave pattern and we certainly have two of the rules in place. The start of my count *did not* begin at the major low indicated on figure 6.1. It started on the intermediate low in September 2004. A purist might cringe at this but as far as I am concerned it stuck out, it met the rules and it suited my time frame. Incidentally, the trigger for the third wave's high was the stock going ex dividend — the gap in prices just below the high represents the ex dividend amount.

All I needed to do at this point was wait out the corrective fourth wave and then join the party for the wave-five high. This is where our guidelines from chapter 5 start to come into play. Guideline three suggested that wave four tends to retrace between 30 per cent and 50 per cent of wave three. The retracement to the wave-four low was 36.09 per cent of the length of wave three — and was also just $0.07 from the 38.2 per cent Fibonacci level. (Fibonacci levels will be covered in chapter 9.) Further, it was just a few cents shy of guideline five — where wave C and wave A tend to be equidistant. These two factors are a strong indicator of a price change. For now, the breakout into new highs allows us to see the count more clearly, as shown in figure 6.2.

Figure 6.3 (on page 91) shows a weekly chart of RMD. As you can see, price action is very choppy and really doesn't exhibit any wave counts — or, at least, none that stands out without it being forced.

Figure 6.4 (on page 92) is also a chart of RMD, but this time it is the daily chart. Positive news from the company saw the price jump through the intermediate high after gapping up. Good news followed by price gapping was the sign for me to pay attention. From there, a nice A-B-C correction can be seen, where wave C was almost exactly equal to the length of wave A. Guideline two was also met as the retracement down from wave one was just over 62 per cent — yet again very close to the Fibonacci 61.8 per cent level.

Adaptive Analysis for Australian Stocks

Figure 6.2: a breakout into new highs

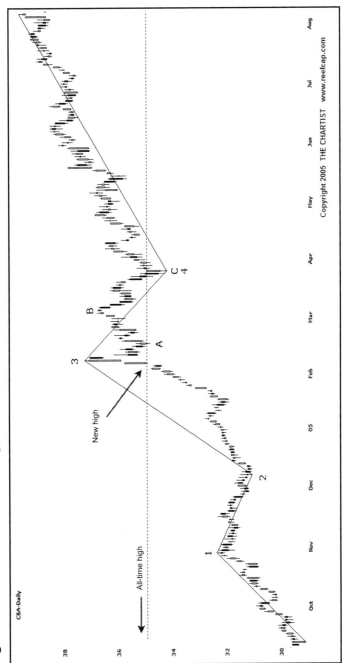

Figure 6.3: Sloppy price action with no simple wave count

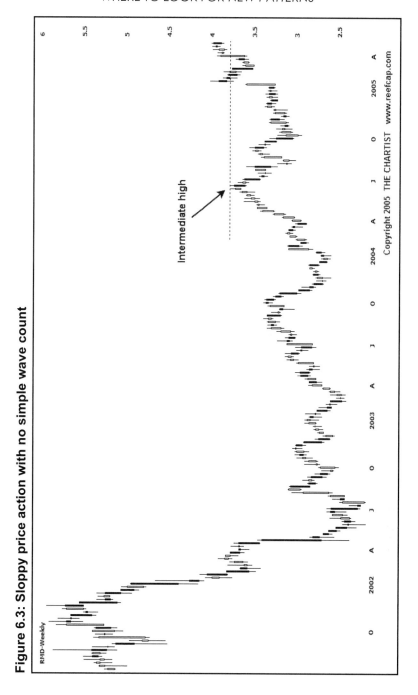

Figure 6.4: multiple factors pointing to a new high

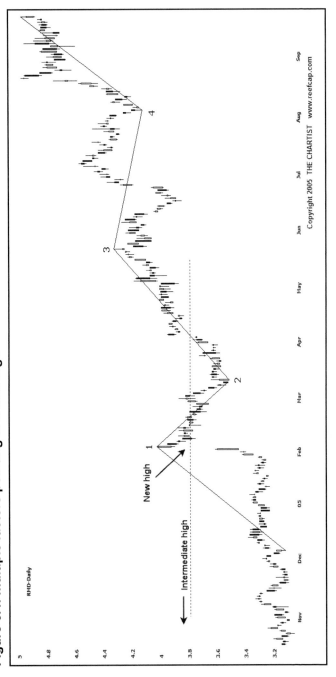

Added to this, the gap on the way up was nicely filled on the way back down. Those not familiar with gaps should take note because they are extremely important indicators. For the most part, markets don't like gaps, so we should expect a gap to be filled before price resumes in the direction of the trend. All these factors — the break to new recent highs, an equidistant three-wave decline, a 62 per cent retracement and the gap fill — all added weight to the wave-two decline being followed by an impulsive third wave to new highs.

As another example, the weekly chart of ASX in figure 6.5 shows an extended period of consolidation. While it is easy to see the two separate areas of price action, impulsive followed by corrective, the second period would be pure guesswork and fraught with danger or frustration for the trader. The chart shows a four-year period of almost no net growth — perhaps a period where funds could have been better utilised in a moving stock. In this scenario, we should wait for a defined breakout, which would certainly confirm that a third wave would be under way.

Figure 6.5: a consolidating stock with no clear patterns

As shown in figure 6.6, a breakout occurred in 2003, after which a retest took place. This was the optimal time to look for a structure. In this example, though, the retracement cannot indicate a wave four because the so-called wave three did not meet rule two — that is, that wave three is usually the longest, but can never be the shortest. Instead, we should firstly view the breakout into new territory as positive price action, then assign a new five-wave pattern as part of the expected larger wave three that is potentially being constructed. In this new count, the waves would be the first and second waves. For this to be correct we should expect the next wave (wave iii) to be at least the same length as the initial wave i, or rise by more than $7.13.

Figure 6.7 (on page 96) shows the outcome as at the time of writing. Indeed, wave iii rose by $8.13, longer than wave i. Wave iv retraced but did not breach the high achieved by wave i. This also means the scope of the larger wave three now aligns itself with wave one and so continues to prove the rules.

The weekly chart of NAB in figure 6.8 (on page 97) shows a break of a multi-year trend line — a perfect place to start looking for a count. As at the time of writing, I have only been able to label waves one and two; however, this has set me up to watch for other smaller patterns on the daily chart.

It is imperative to look for any point a wave count and subsequent pattern can form. A pattern need not complete itself in order for me to make a profit, so perfect theory is not at the top of my agenda.

Figure 6.6: a defined breakout after consolidation

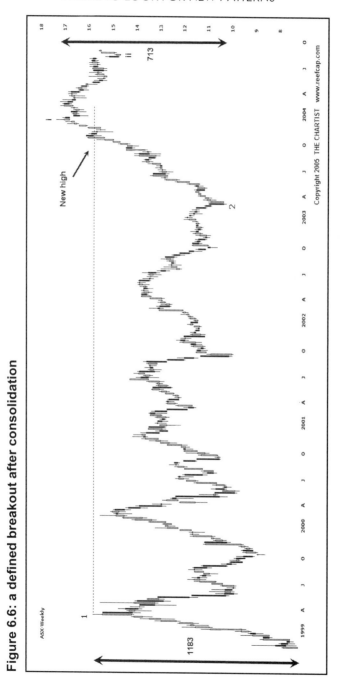

Figure 6.7: patterns emerging after consolidation

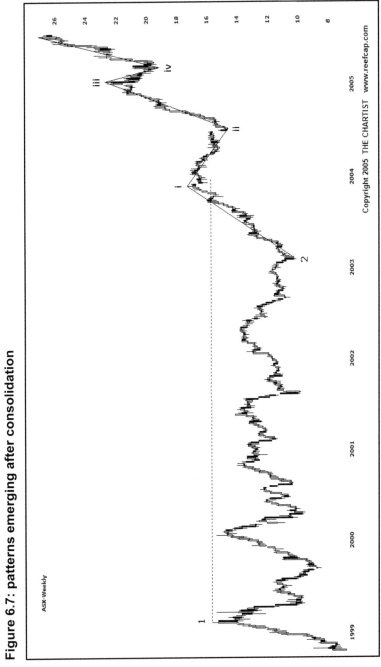

Figure 6.8: breakout of a multi-year trendline

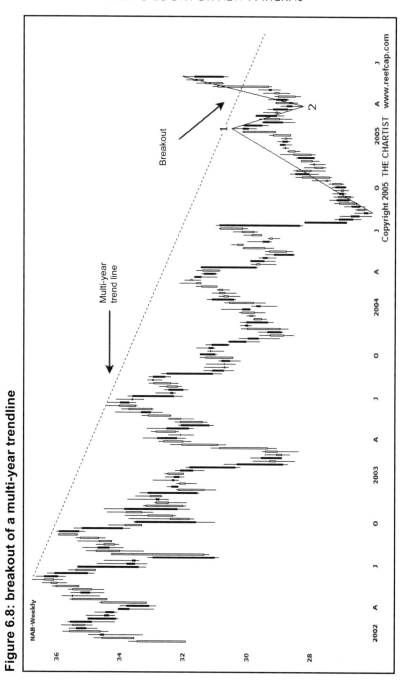

CHAPTER 7

RAW WAVE TRADING — PART I

Before moving onto steps two and three of the trading process, you might be interested in how you can trade the market swings discussed in chapter 6 just on their own. As far as I am aware, the following technique is completely original and was introduced through my newsletter in March 2004. This simple mechanism allows an entry point to be defined after the price starts to turn around — in other words, rather than attempting to buy as prices decline, you only buy after they have turned up and momentum is starting to rise in your favour again. You don't need to define specific Elliott waves to use it, however.

Determining the entry point

Figure 7.1 shows a completed five-wave pattern in Coles Myer Ltd (CML). Firstly, we're going to focus on the first and second waves. Because wave three is the longest wave, if we could combine both waves three and five, it should offer the best profit potential. As you can see from the chart, the entire set of core EW rules were met.

Figure 7.1: CML showing a completed EW pattern

Figure 7.2 is a close-up view of waves one and two shown above. The horizontal lines divide wave one into equal segments, in this case fifths. You may select any segment size you wish. The more segments, the lower the risk but the higher the chance of getting stopped out in market noise. I find fifths and quarters tend to provide a good balance.

The entry mechanism requires prices to dip below one of the segment lines and then move back above the next highest segment line. As can be seen in figure 7.2, after the high of wave one, there are three days where the 20 per cent segment line is broken. To get an entry, prices must rise back above the next highest line (in this case, the 0 per cent); however, it failed to materialise. On the fourth day, prices dipped below the 40 per cent line — as marked on the chart at 'X'. To buy, the price must now travel back above the 20 per cent line, as this is now the next highest segment. This occurred the next day, as marked at 'Y'. My interpretation of this situation is that prices now have positive momentum and that the wave-two decline may have been completed — of course, we can never know for sure. As the entry mechanism has been triggered, the trade should be entered as soon as the 20 per cent segment line is breached. The protective stop should be placed just below the wave-two low.

Figure 7.2: wave one divided into five segments

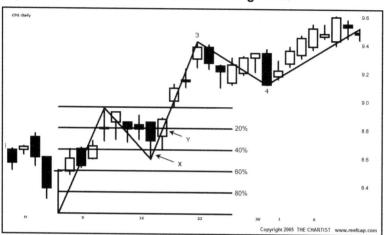

In this example, you would buy when prices break through $8.80 and then place the protective stop at $8.58, just below the $8.59 low at the bottom of wave two. As at writing, prices in CML have travelled to $9.60 — providing an unrealised $0.80 profit for an initial risk of $0.22.

The next example shows the versatility of the mechanism in that it can be applied to any time frame — in this case, a weekly chart. It also shows the huge profit potential if these larger waves are captured. In the example shown, prices rose by 100 per cent.

As shown in figure 7.3, Coates Hire Ltd (COA) rose off a major low in late 2001. By the end of 2002, a sizeable decline was under way, suggesting a possible second wave.

Figure 7.3: a five-wave pattern unfolding (COA weekly chart)

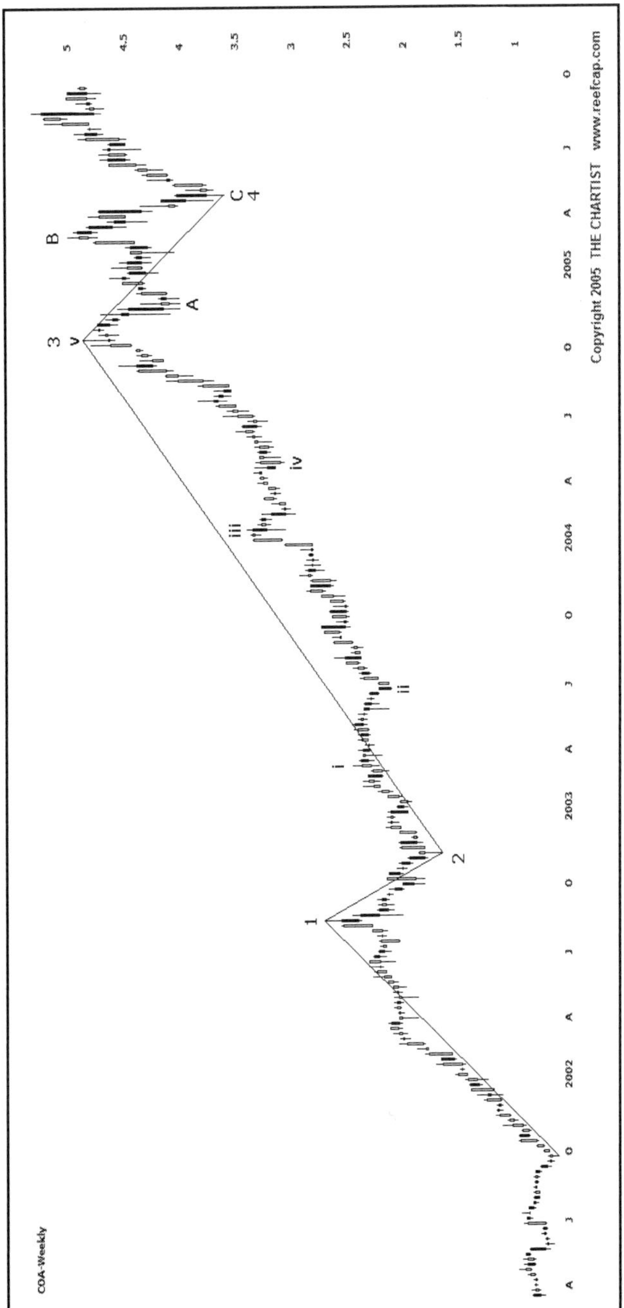

COA-Weekly

Copyright 2005 THE CHARTIST www.reefcap.com

On closer inspection, the 40 per cent segment line after the initial high was breached on two occasions, as shown in figure 7.4. The first failed to move back through the 20 per cent trigger level, but the second time prices started to rise they broke up through the buy level. Once again, as soon as the entry mechanism is triggered, a protective stop should be placed just below the most recent low.

Figure 7.4: wave one divided into five segments with entry mechanism triggered

The entry mechanism described above is a very simplified model for trading any swings. Adding the EW theory, though, allows you to understand better the depths of retracements and the length of the impulsive trends. It is not a foolproof method — nothing is — but it allows you to trade in the direction of the trend, allows a low-risk entry and offers a plan that can be replicated across any time frame you choose.

The chart of Australian Pharmaceutical Industries Ltd (API) shown in figure 7.5 is another typical example.

Figure 7.5: API showing an explosive move

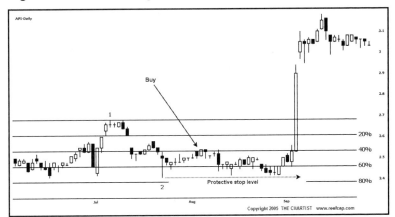

Let's talk through the activity as it occurred:

- *7 July 2004* — reaches high of $2.68, marked as wave one
- *14 July 2004* — declines down through 20 per cent and 40 per cent segments
- *21 July 2004* — prices push back through 40 per cent but unable to cross 20 per cent line
- *23 July 2004* —declines further to $2.41; 40 per cent and 60 per cent segments breached
- *4 August 2004* — prices push to a high of $2.53, crossing the 40 per cent segment at $2.52 and activating a buy signal; the protective stop is placed below the 23 July low at $2.40, meaning the risk is $0.12
- *31 August 2004* — after several weeks of sideways trading, prices decline again and halt at $2.42; the protective stop at $2.40 remains intact
- *6 September 2004* — prices rocket to $2.94
- *14 September 2004* — momentum continues to push prices higher, reaching $3.18.

At this stage, prices have moved $0.66 from the entry. With an initial risk of $0.12, the potential risk/reward is over five. This example may be construed as simple luck — the market drifted sideways for some time and another test of the lows just missed activating the protective stop. So be it, but this highlights a basic entry technique that allows a low-risk entry.

Pyramiding the position

On some occasions, long-term moves covering the full EW pattern can be caught using this method. The following weekly charts in ASX show how we can initiate a position within wave two and follow it up with another pyramid position in wave four.

Figure 7.6 shows a close-up of the first and second waves just after all-time highs were made in October 2004. Using our rules and guidelines from chapter 5, we know that second waves tend to be deep and usually retrace beyond the 50 per cent level; however, in this instance that was not the case. Experience suggests to me that if wave two's retracement *is not* deep, there are two possibilities to consider — either the count is incorrect, or the trend is extremely strong and any dips are well sort by buyers. Over the last few years I have noticed an increase in the latter scenario — which is obviously associated with the bull market mentality seen over this period. Failing to realise this meant I missed opportunities — for example, Aristocrat (ALL), which went onto triple in price while I waited for the second wave to retrace to the desired level. Since then, and while the market retains its bullish stance, I tend to look to enter wave two prematurely. I might be wrong on occasion, but the upside potential is too great to miss out on.

Because ASX hit all-time highs and then pulled back to retest that breakout (a very common occurrence), there was always a chance that wave two would be shallow. As can be seen in figure 7.6, it just dipped past the 30 per cent retracement of wave one.

Figure 7.6: a shallow wave two

As soon as you're confident that some kind of new corrective wave is taking place, you can look to enter in the direction of the main trend. As new lows are made each day, simply use the 20 per cent segments to define the entry point.

Figure 7.7 shows the segment lines at 60 per cent, 80 per cent and 100 per cent — with the 100 per cent segment line eventually becoming the wave-two low. The 80 per cent segment line is also the 30 per cent retracement point of wave one and as such is the time to start looking for a second wave. In this particular trade, I entered prematurely and was stopped out as wave two continued lower. The 80 per cent segment line was breached, followed by the 60 per cent entry line, so I entered the trade and was long at $15.77. I was then stopped out as prices reversed and continued lower, so I realised a loss of $0.55.

Two days later, prices jumped back through the 80 per cent segment line at $15.22 (my second entry point, marked on the chart as buy #2) and never looked back. At that stage, I was riding the strongest part of the trend, wave three, and was also aware that wave four would eventuate at some point. In this situation, you need to decide whether you intend to exit near the high of wave three and re-enter the trade during wave four, or just ride out wave four when it occurs. If you decide to exit near the high of wave three, a simple trailing stop such as a moving average is the easiest way to protect against the fourth wave eating away at too much of your profit.

Figure 7.7: trade re-entered after initially being stopped out

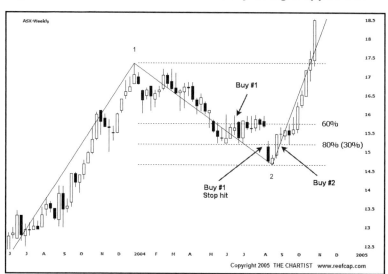

Figure 7.8 (overleaf) shows the long third wave that took prices toward $23.00 before wave four started. Remember — you can never know how far prices will travel or when wave four will start, but you can always be prepared for it.

As seen in the initial entry in wave two, our 20 per cent segment lines just provided enough noise for the first attempt at pyramiding to be stopped out. The losses from both the initial purchase and the third were very small in comparison to the possible gains, so a few similar buys really will not harm you. In buy number three, the loss was about $0.80, making the total losses from the two false signals $1.35. However, the gain from buy number two was well over $5.00 at this point.

Figure 7.8: pyramiding the initial position using wave four

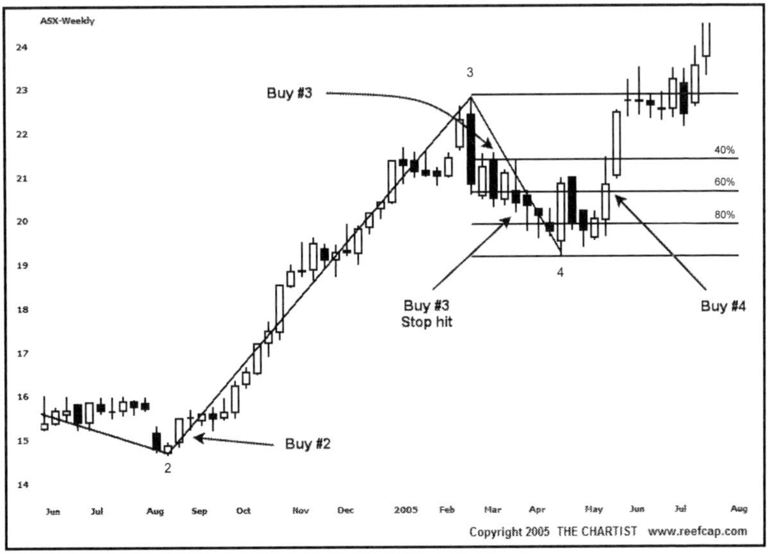

Several weeks later the 80 per cent segment line from the high of wave three was broken again and was then followed by a rampaging bullish week that enabled buy number four to be activated at $20.61. The stop at $19.20 held through a few nervous weeks before the trend, and therefore wave five, resumed. As at the time of writing, the stock is over $25.50 and I expect prices to continue to move toward $26.50.

In review:

- Buy #1   −$0.55
- Buy #2   +$10.28 (basis $25.50, unrealised)
- Buy #3   −$0.80
- Buy #4   +$4.89 (basis $25.50, unrealised)
- Total   +13.82.

CHAPTER 8

RAW WAVE
TRADING — PART II

The method outlined in this chapter is slightly more complex than the method discussed in chapter 7; however, it can offer some great rewards for the patient trader or someone who really doesn't wish to watch the market closely. It is based on the theory of the three-wave corrections that are commonly seen in EW. Many methods attempt to trade around these corrections because they tend to be followed by strong impulsive waves — for example, two vendor-based patterns that I am aware of are Wolfe waves and Butterflies. A software program that is designed to look for these as well is MTPredictor™. The theme I outline here is slightly different from these systems and it can put the odds in your favour very quickly.

Figure 8.1 shows the swings in the price action of CBA that are more than 10 per cent in length. The point of this method is to buy near the low of the last swing (in this case, down near $23.05) and then take profits at the absolute high (here, at $34.94). The size of the swing used is also important. I tend to use 10 per cent for most stocks, but lower priced stocks will require a higher percentage — for example, a $5 stock will need a 15 per cent swing, and an even lower priced stock will need 20 per cent. This is really the only discretionary part of the set-up.

Figure 8.1: a three-wave correction following an all-time high

Entering during a correction — the rules

The first rule for this entry method is that we must always trade in the direction of the major trend. The overall trend for CBA is clearly up because all-time highs were seen in mid-2002, followed by a 34 per cent corrective move that formed the three waves. The swings highlighted in figure 8.1 are of 10 per cent or more. Any smaller swings did not meet the 10 per cent criterion and therefore were not labelled by the computer.

The second rule is that you should only take a trade if the reward is at least 2.5 times the initial risk. You may adjust this as you see fit, but I will personally not go below 2.5 times. The way to calculate this ratio will become obvious once I explain the entry. To determine the exit point, a profit target is set at the start of the corrective move — so in this example, profits will be taken at $34.94, as long as prices return to that level.

If you are using a 10 per cent swing, the entry point will be a 10 per cent swing off the low point, or off the end of wave C as we now know it. As can be seen in figure 8.1, wave C ends at $23.05; therefore, the entry will be made if prices travel back up through $25.35 ($23.05 × 1.10). As prices move lower, you should keep calculating the new entry level until the trend has reversed by the 10 per cent amount.

The protective stop will be placed just below the major low — in this case, at $23.04. If you enter at $25.35 and place the protective stop at $23.04, the risk will therefore be $2.31. The profit target is $34.94, so the reward will be $9.59 ($34.94 – $25.35) compared to the risk of $2.31. Hence, the risk/reward ratio is 4.15 ($9.59 ÷ $2.31). Going back to the expectancy curve from chapter 1, this is very acceptable.

Figure 8.2 (overleaf) shows the outcome after two years — as I said earlier, this style is for the patient trader or active investor. The capital gain is 37.8 per cent over the two-year holding period. During this time, $3.38 in dividends were also distributed, taking the total return to 51 per cent.

It's important to remember that the entry point can be determined well in advance and therefore you will also know where to place the protective stop and whether or not the reward to risk ratio is acceptable. You will see this set-up quite often, but the reward to risk ratio will not always be favourable. Don't be tempted to take a trade simply because you see the A-B-C correction. Wait till the odds are in your favour.

Waiting till the odds are in your favour

The next example, shown in figure 8.3 on page 113, is Patrick Corporation Ltd (PRK) again using a weekly chart with the swings set to 15 per cent. The trend was firmly up when prices hit $5.92 in mid-2002. This was followed by a three-wave decline to a low of $3.95. The problem here was that a 15 per cent swing from $3.95 produced a reward/risk ratio that was barely 2.0, so no trade could be entered as prices spiked to $5.14.

Figure 8.2: CBA trend over two years

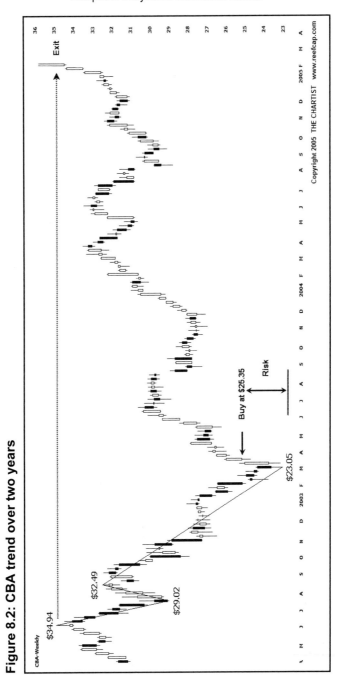

Figure 8.3: the trend for PRK

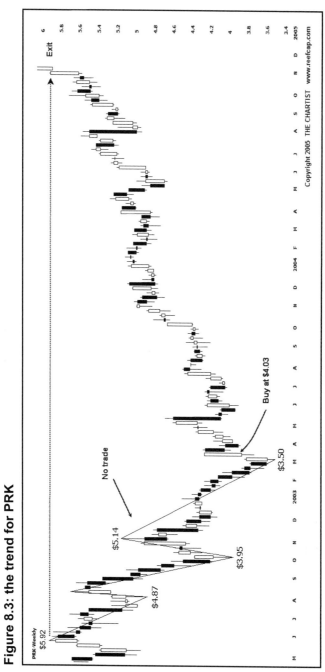

From the price spike at $5.14, prices then tumbled to a low of $3.50, almost 41 per cent lower than the peak of $5.92 in early 2002. The potential reward was now substantially higher at 3.5 times the risk. The entry point — at a 15 per cent swing higher from the major low — was $4.03. With a protective stop placed at $3.49, the risk was $0.54. If prices made it to the target of $5.92, the profit would be $1.89. The risk/reward is therefore aligned to preferred levels. During the holding period, $0.34 worth of dividends were paid, taking the total profit to $2.23 or 55.3 per cent for the 20 months.

The price action for IINet Ltd (IIN) in figure 8.4 showed a three-wave decline of some 35 per cent in late 2003 to early 2004. Like Patrick, the entry was based on a 15 per cent swing from the $2.21 low in early 2004, meaning in this case the entry was $2.54 ($2.21 × 1.15). The initial risk was $0.34 and a target of $3.40 made the ratio 2.52, which just met my minimum criterion. Profits were taken 12 months later at $3.40 (the point where the initial correction started). Added to the $0.86 in capital growth was $0.07 in dividends, making the total return 36.6 per cent — not too bad for a year's worth of patience.

Figure 8.4: IIN's 36.6 per cent gain

Keep the risk/reward ratio as wide as possible

Like every part of trading, you will not always be right using this method. So long as you keep the possible risk/reward ratio as wide as possible, however, you will succeed — over time. The trend for Fortescue Metals Group Ltd (FMG), shown in figure 8.5, is a good example of a trade where I was a little unlucky, but the risk/reward was so high, I could afford to take a few shots at it.

Figure 8.5: the risk/reward offered by FMG

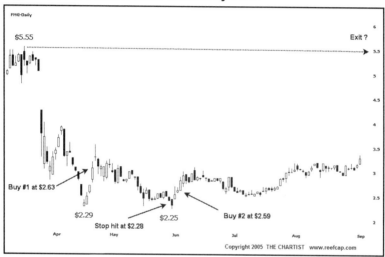

Using a 15 per cent swing, prices could be seen to correct down to $2.29 in an A-B-C move. A buy was activated at $2.63 ($2.29 × 1.15). Once the buy was activated, a protective stop was placed at $2.28. Unfortunately, this meant I was just stopped out of the trade a few months later. The trade set-up, however, remained in place from that second low at $2.25, meaning I was able to re-enter at $2.59. As at the time of writing, the current situation is as follows:

- Buy #1 $0.35
- Buy #2   +$0.71 (basis $3.30, unrealised)
- Total   +$0.36
- Target total +$2.96 (basis $5.55, theoretical).

The theoretical profit means the risk/reward ratio is extremely high at 8.45 — although, of course, you can never know whether or not it will be achieved. So far so good, but there is a long way to go. Another consideration is that FMG does not pay any dividends so I am not being paid while waiting for the target to be achieved. In this situation, it might be worthwhile adding a 'premium' to the minimum risk/reward ratio required in order to better amplify the profits.

Recognising the patterns in real-time

The next example shows how these patterns form in real-time and how you know when the odds are in your favour. On 5 September 2005, Telstra Corporation Ltd (TLS) suggested that earnings might be lower than expected. Prices were sold off heavily and closed the day at $4.34. As at the time of writing, TLS's low of $3.92 made in early 2003 was its lowest point since listing. My view is that if that low breaks, the door is open for more downside and a continuance of the pathetic price action that has been seen over the recent years.

In light of this, it makes sense that $3.92 be a prudent place for a protective stop. I don't think anyone should get too excited about the prospects of TLS until the government's involvement is resolved — and how long that will take is anybody's guess. Again, taking current circumstances into account, I believe it is unlikely prices will exceed the highs of early 2005 in the near future. The current risk/reward if prices did go back to these highs is shown in figure 8.6.

There is now a protective stop level and an estimated profit target. If you were to buy at today's prices, the risk/reward ratio would be 2.6 — nothing special really, considering the current mood toward the stock, and the fact that you're buying it on the way down rather than waiting for momentum to reverse upward. However, if TLS pays another $0.40 worth of dividends while you wait for prices to return to the target (as it did in the previous 12 months), the risk/reward ratio moves out to 3.6. That is getting better.

Figure 8.6: Seeing the pattern in real time

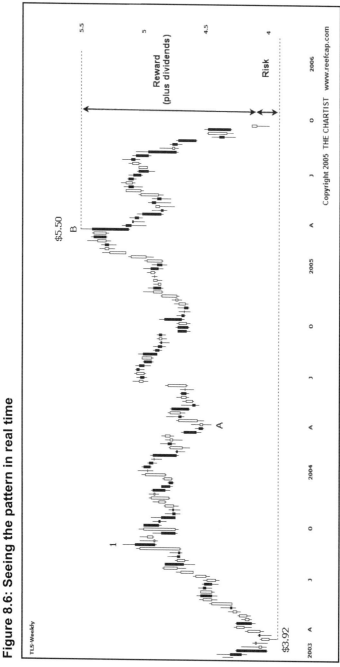

TLS-Weekly

$5.50

$3.92

Reward
(plus dividends)

Risk

B

A

1

5.5

5

4.5

4

2003 A J O 2004 A J O 2005 A J O 2006

Copyright 2005 THE CHARTIST www.reefcap.com

What if you got greedy? After all, you are buying as prices decline, so perhaps you should add some premium onto your risk/reward ratio. The further TLS declines toward $3.92, the higher your risk/reward gets, so the question starts to become do you buy on the way down and increase the risk/reward ratio to very favourable levels, or do you wait for further declines and then a reversal of momentum to offer some confirmation? The answer to this question really comes down to your own comfort level. One option means buying while prices are falling, but offers greater rewards. The other option means buying when (if) prices start to rise again, which offers a small element of positive confirmation but also removes some of the reward.

What will occur? Who knows and nobody can know. According to the Aspect Financial <www.aspectfinancial.com.au> analyst consensus data at the time of writing, two brokers have 'strong buy' recommendations, one has 'moderate buy', 11 have 'hold', one has 'moderate sell' and one has 'strong sell'. It's clear from this that those who study fundamental analysis don't have any idea either. Once again, my point is that I am not concerned with whether I am right or wrong. All I know is that if I am right, the reward I will receive will far outweigh the risk I am taking. If I am to do this over the longer term, I will always come out a profitable trader.

As you can see, this method is reasonably rule-based, which means it can be tested on past data and replicated into the future. All you're really doing is setting some boundaries for a high win/loss ratio that enables your trading to remain well above the expectancy curve. Most software packages available these days have the ability to show these swings. A list of the coding required for the popular software packages is provided in the appendices.

CHAPTER 9

STEP TWO — IDENTIFYING CONFLUENCE

Confluence — an intersection of two or more points; a coming together of various elements.[1]

So far I've looked at my philosophy of profitable trading and how to use what is arguably the most advanced technique to define trends within step one of the trading process. You're halfway there, and what I'm about to outline here, step two, is extremely important for exploiting those trends even further and helping to ensure better entry timing.

I don't use EW at just any old time to enter a trade — I also require the theory to be supported by a factor known as confluence. When analysing the markets it is important to find areas where several elements of the chart more or less meet. It is at these areas of confluence that more pieces of the puzzle come together, as they can indicate areas where change may take place. Hence, areas of confluence can be very important. I use EW as the trend identifier and confluence as a point of reference to take a closer look at price action before applying step three.

We're able to combine the rules and guidelines of the Elliott principle from chapter 5 with other simple chart points — such as highs and

---

1   Source: <www.dictionary.com>.

lows, Fibonacci levels, definable patterns, support and resistance, or other tools we deem important. Personally, I stay with price relationships and patterns that occur at those points rather than use indicators, but you may wish to investigate your own ideas. Many experts use time factors as well, but I'm yet to find a way to add that dimension and be comfortable with it.

Let's look at some classic examples of confluence at work on ASX stocks. In order to better discuss the theory behind some of these points of confluence, I'll first introduce the basic application of Fibonacci. Like Elliott wave theory, information relating to Fibonacci can be found extensively on the internet.

Fibonacci levels

Fibonacci, or more correctly Leonardo da Pisa, was born in Pisa in 1175. Fibonacci is perhaps best known for a simple series of numbers, named the Fibonacci sequence. The series begins with 0 and 1. It then continues with: 2, 3, 5, 8, 13, 21, 34, 55, 89, 144, 233, 377, 610, 987, and so on. To create this sequence, there are some simple rules:

- The sum of any two consecutive numbers equals the next highest number. For example, 1 + 2 = 3; 2 + 3 = 5; 3 + 5 = 8; and so on.

- If you take the ratios of successive Fibonacci numbers — 1/2, 2/3, 3/5, 5/8, 8/13, 13/21, 21/34, and so on — the fractions get closer and closer to the golden ratio (or golden section) 'R', which is about 0.61803.

- The ratio of any number to its next lowest number is approximately 1.618 — the inverse of the golden ratio.

The golden ratio is a very special number, and has been known about since Greek times. Paintings with a height to width ratio of this number have an especially aesthetically pleasing aspect. The Parthenon in Athens uses the same ratio. The five-pointed stars on many flags of the world (for example, the flag used by the European

Union) are made by cutting the diagonals of a pentagon according to the golden ratio. The ratio is sometimes called the 'divine proportion', which is particularly apt as many religious paintings also use it.

The surprising thing about Fibonacci's sequence is that it occurs in nature as well as in the markets. The way in which the spiral patterns of sunflower seeds and pine cones grow is described by the sequence, and it is common for the number of petals on a flower to be a Fibonacci number. Four-leaved clovers are rarer than five-leaved ones because five is in Fibonacci's sequence and four isn't!

Fibonacci and trading

So why is the Fibonacci number sequence important to trading, especially when applying the Elliott wave theory? There are two reasons.

Firstly, when looking at the wave counts you will see that a complete sequence consists of eight waves — three waves up and two waves down to form the five impulsive waves, and then two waves down to one wave up to form the three corrective waves. Eight is a Fibonacci number, as are one, two, three and five. As the waves subdivide, they do so at the rate of the ongoing Fibonacci sequence.

Secondly, the proportion of wave relationships, both corrective and impulsive, also show tendencies toward the Fibonacci ratios. Corrective waves are also known as retracements — that is, prices retrace back on themselves. One of the most common retracements is 50 per cent or 0.50. This is the Fibonacci ratio 1/2. The other two common retracement levels are 61.8 per cent (13/21) and 38.2 per cent, which is the reciprocal of 61.8 per cent. When looking at expanding or impulsive moves, Fibonacci relationships can again be found. For example, the end of wave three tends to be 61.8 per cent of the length of wave one from the high point of wave one. Also, the end of wave five tends to be a combination of wave three multiplied by 61.8 per cent and wave one multiplied by 1.618 per cent.

Using the Fibonacci sequence, some recent examples of confluence will now be discussed.

Examples of confluence

One of the most recent examples of confluence occurred in CML. Figure 9.1 shows five elements that came together more or less at the same level to suggest that wave (4) was at an important intersection. These were:

1 The level of the high point of wave (1) was approaching and it needed to hold — one of the core rules.

2 The level for what had been a clear resistance line during a 10-week sideways pattern, which became support on the way back down.

3 The length of wave (C) in relation to the length of wave (A), one of the guidelines.

4 The point of a 38.2 per cent Fibonacci retracement of the complete move from the start of the trend to the end of wave (3).

5 The point of a 61.8 per cent Fibonacci retracement of wave (3).

All five of these elements intersected very close to the same level. Rarely, if at all, will they meet at exactly the same point — but as a trader, I'm not looking for perfection, I'm looking for profits. Also noticeable is the classic blow-off bottom on the exact low of wave (4), which was also a good sign that negative price action was losing momentum. As at the time of writing, CML has rallied 17 per cent in just a few weeks as part of the larger wave (5).

In the next example, shown in figure 9.2 on page 124, there are early signs of confluence in the price action of Colorado Group Ltd (CDO). Again, this was at a wave-four low, but this time prices also exhibited a traditional bullish pattern.

Figure 9.1: confluence at wave (4) in CML weekly chart

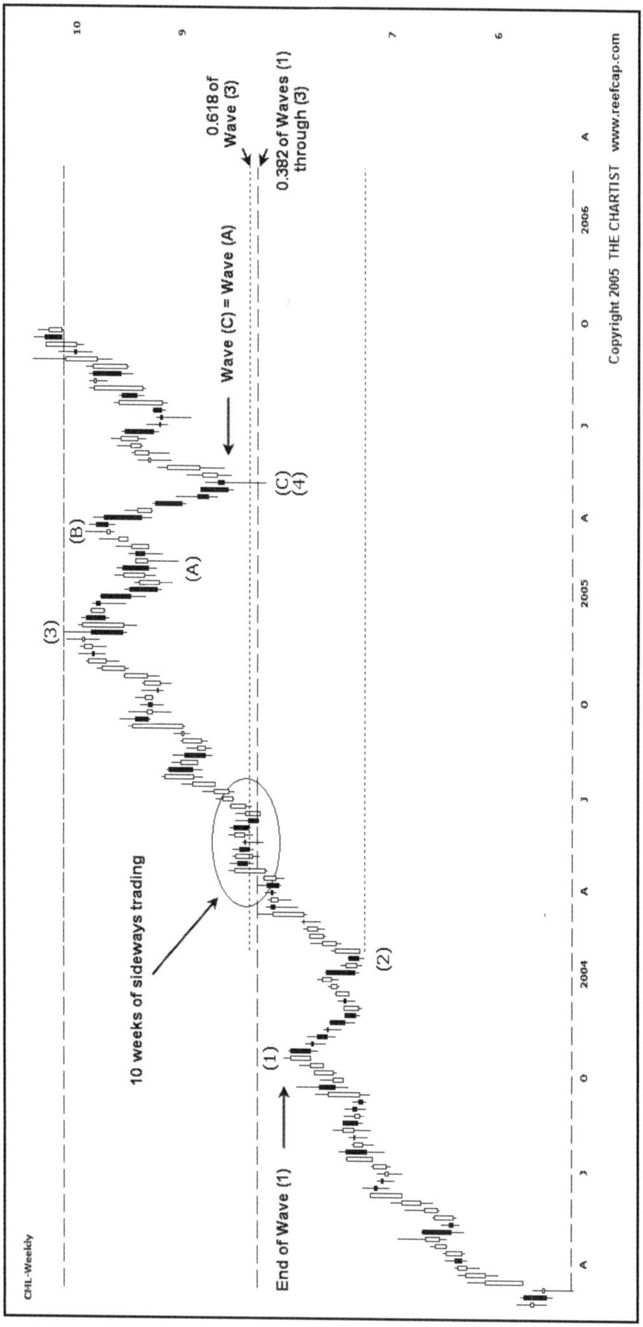

CML-Weekly

10 weeks of sideways trading

End of Wave (1)

(1)

(2)

(3)

(A)

(B)

(C)
(4)

Wave (C) = Wave (A)

0.618 of Wave (3)

0.382 of Waves (1) through (3)

2004   2005   2006

Copyright 2005 THE CHARTIST   www.reefcap.com

Figure 9.2: confluence at wave four in CDO weekly chart

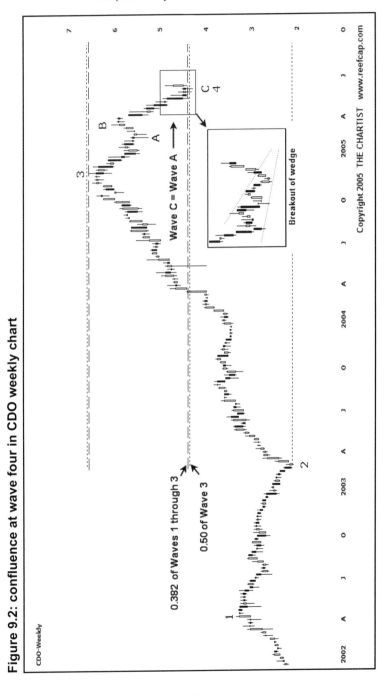

CDO-Weekly

Wave C = Wave A

0.382 of Waves 1 through 3

0.50 of Wave 3

Breakout of wedge

Copyright 2005 THE CHARTIST www.reefcap.com

The points of confluence are:

- A 38.2 per cent Fibonacci retracement of the complete move from the start of the trend to the end of wave three.

- A 50 per cent Fibonacci retracement of wave three.

- The length of wave C in relation to the length of wave A, one of the guidelines.

The formation and consequent breakout of a falling wedge pattern also occurred exactly at the point of the Fibonacci levels. A falling wedge is a classical pattern that tends to forewarn of a price increase.

It is early days for CDO and by the time this book goes to print I may have been proven wrong; however, if this is the start of wave five, the risk/reward potential is very high and that is all I'm after as a trader.

The next example of confluence, shown in figure 9.3 overleaf, is a weekly chart of Jumbuck Entertainment Ltd (JBM). There are three levels of confluence:

1   A retracement to and retest of a major high.

2   A 50 per cent Fibonacci retracement of wave three.

3   Four tests of the old high, which created a major new support level.

As can be seen, the last wave, wave five, is subdividing into a smaller degree pattern that should take prices well through $7.00.

Figure 9.3: confluence at wave four in JBM weekly chart

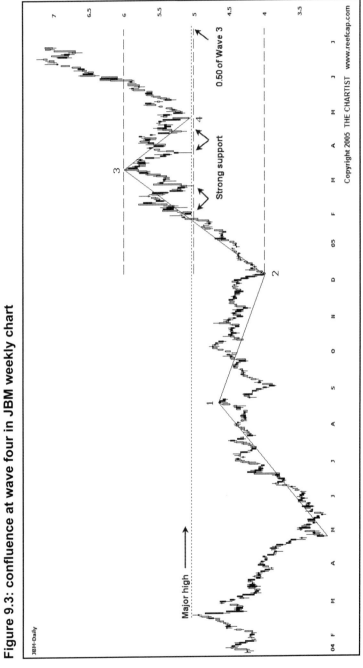

Confluence is also apparent in much larger time frames — it can sometimes just take a bit of research to see it. The monthly chart of Brambles Industries Ltd (BIL) in figure 9.4 shows a massive downtrend lasting several years, where prices declined from $13.00 to below $4.00. The bounce that followed shows three points of confluence on this time frame. They are:

1   An exact 50 per cent retracement of the multi-year decline.

2   A resistance level at the last major low made in 2000, where priced have now halted.

3   The last major low is also the point where the retracement has completed a five-wave pattern up. Within this pattern, wave five and wave one were just $0.01 apart in length (meeting guideline four).

Figure 9.4: monthly confluence in BIL chart

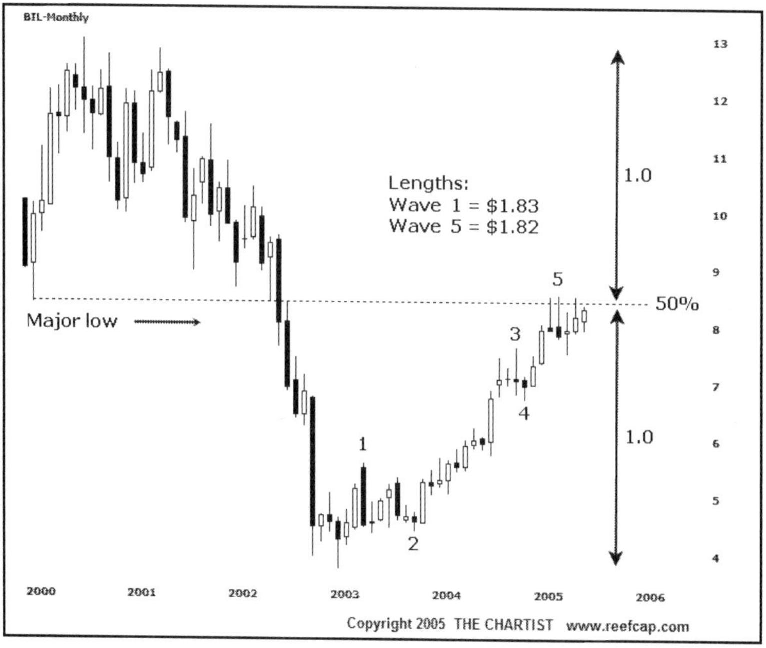

Will BIL reverse from here in an A-B-C pattern? Only time will tell. On very special occasions, you'll see confluence on large time frames, such as seen with BIL, and on smaller time frames. It is at these times that the market is almost begging you to participate.

Keep an eye out for areas of confluence because it can certainly add weight to a probable change of trend and your decision to enter the market.

CHAPTER 10

STEP THREE — FINDING LOW-RISK MICRO PATTERNS

Regardless of the market or time frame, your trading toolbox should only contain the tools required to fulfil the very simple concept of finding, interpreting and trading low-risk patterns. Curtis Arnold introduced me to such a theory in 1995 after I read his book *PPS Trading System* (Irwin Professional Publishing, 1989), and this has been a major part of my trading arsenal ever since, especially in the futures markets where I concentrated most of my efforts until CFDs were introduced. These patterns can be found in any market and on any time frame. They usually offer extremely specific low-risk entries, high enough frequency to be of immense value and can be traded with or against the trend. Obviously, these patterns can vary between simple and advanced. I tend to use very simple and very small patterns that I call micro patterns. I apply them with very specific rules to ensure I know when and where to enter and exit. A micro pattern is no different to normal textbook patterns such as triangles, flags, double bottoms and tops, and congestions. However, micro patterns are small, usually lasting just eight to twelve days, as opposed to classic patterns that can last weeks or months. In some circumstances, these micro patterns can last less than four days.

It is important at this juncture to remind you that the patterns I outline from here on are simply tools. These patterns do not make the money; they are simply offering a very low-risk way of entering the market. If you would rather use an RSI or some other indicator, go right ahead — but, first and foremost, ensure you understand why the profits are being generated. The indicator — or in my case, the pattern — is the tool. It makes sense to me and is something I am able to relate to. If I can relate to the trade set-up and feel comfortable with it, I am better prepared to follow it through, execute my entry and obey my protective stop. However, I also intimately know that the reason I am profitable is because I am using low-risk entries and allowing the profits to run. These combined skew the win/loss ratio in my favour.

Consolidation patterns

Quite possibly the easiest pattern to recognise on any time frame is a flat congestion area. You may be aware of the concept of a 'Darvas box' or have read Darvas's book *How I Made $2,000,000 in the Stockmarket* (Carol Publishing Corporation, 1986). If you haven't, buy a copy for a simple and enjoyable holiday read. (Essentially, Darvas would establish a so-called box, or trading range. If the stock broke out on the upside, he would buy, especially if the breakout was accompanied by large volume. After a breakout, Darvas would use a trailing stop to ensure that he locked in most of his profit, while giving the market sufficient room to make normal retracements without the stop being triggered. If the stock broke below the box, his stop loss order would be hit and he would take a small loss.) If you are familiar with the Darvas box and now understand my philosophy, can you see what Darvas was doing? He was simply following the trend, finding low-risk entries and pyramiding. In other words, he was skewing the numbers in his favour!

I would like to digress a little. If you grasp my approach on basic maths and expectancy, do a Google search for Darvas boxes. The extent to which people have gone to in order to replicate the definition of the box itself is almost laughable. In other words, these people don't understand what's making the money. They think it's the genius of these little boxes and their make-up as opposed to the *real* factors of cutting losses and letting the profits run. This then brings us back to the point of seeing trading in a new light — one where expensive software and heavy-handed salespeople aren't able to offer anything better than what you already have because all they offer is the tools. Agreed — in some instances, certain tools can make the daily routine easier. However, they will not make you a more profitable trader. Before you go out and buy Darvas box software, think about what you are actually buying.

Micro consolidation patterns

Back to the charts and low-risk entry. Reading the market is amazingly simple at times. Figure 10.1, for example, is a situation where a reasonable top was put in place in April 2004. Prices attempted to go higher on several occasions, finally failed and then fell about 15 per cent. It was a slow climb back up and the old highs were eventually overcome. What occurred next is extremely common at old highs — I have been watching this for the last 10 years across all markets and it has been repeated time and time again. What usually occurs next is that prices consolidate in some type of tight or *micro* pattern.

This consolidation usually happens right on the old highs. In the chart of Bluescope Steel Ltd (BSL) shown in figure 10.1, you can see that it occurs just above the highs. Why? Perhaps because many people who bought the recent dip couldn't wait to take profits, or those who were unable to take profits at the last high didn't want to miss out again, as they felt that the old highs would keep prices down again. Hence, the price action becomes a minor 'tug of war' between the old buyers looking for a second chance to get out and take profits, and the new buyers seeking to re-enter after the trend has resumed.

Figure 10.1: trading congestion above support

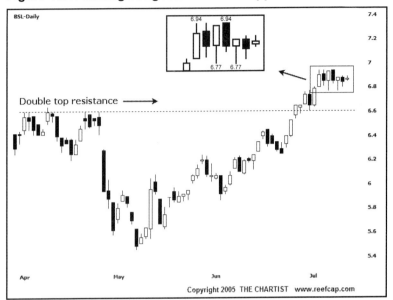

Copyright 2005 THE CHARTIST www.reefcap.com

There are several points to note. The congestion is very small, which enables a low-risk entry. Remember that a low-risk entry is one where the distance from the entry point to the protective stop point is small. These micro congestions offer such a scenario. Also notice that the small range consisted of four internal points. Point one — always in the direction of the trend — was $6.94, followed by a low at $6.77, followed by another push to $6.94 and lastly a retest of $6.77. Watch these micro patterns — most consist of four internal points that can guide you.

Figure 10.2 shows the follow-through price action. Prices broke up through the top of the congestion, indicating that the trend was continuing. Those who exited at the old high (thinking they'd missed the boat) were probably tempted to get back aboard now, which only added further momentum and helped the upward trend. Compare the size of the trend to the entry risk!

Figure 10.2: continuation of the trend after period of congestion

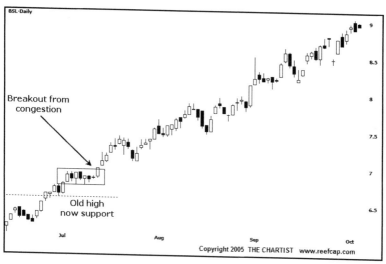

At the time of writing, ASX had recently powered to new all-time highs. It did so after breaking out of a consolidation that occurred at an old high and also consisted of four internal points, as shown in figure 10.3.

Figure 10.3: a familiar pattern of congestion at an old high

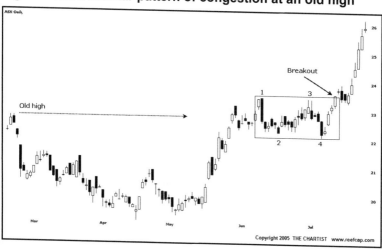

As figure 10.4 shows, at the time of writing Australian Worldwide Exploration Ltd (AWE) had recently consolidated into a small micro box just above a major high. Which way it breaks is yet to be seen.

Figure 10.4: AWE consolidating at old highs

These patterns are just so common that they can be used as a stand-alone tool for low-risk entries. As shown in figure 10.5, Coates Hire Ltd (COA) produced a tight congestion in an ongoing trend — one that at the time of writing is producing new all-time highs.

As shown in figure 10.6 on page 136, Iluka Resources broke to new highs then went into an extended period of consolidation. While there was a large consolidation forming just above an old high, which is an indicator of strong support, prices then contracted into an even smaller consolidation, offering an even lower risk trade. (The protective stop is placed just below the lower boundary line of the congestion.) Prices started to accelerate once the larger box was overcome, but if you'd picked up on the price action in the micro box, you could be already in on the action with even lower risk.

Figure 10.5: COA congests at a new all-time high

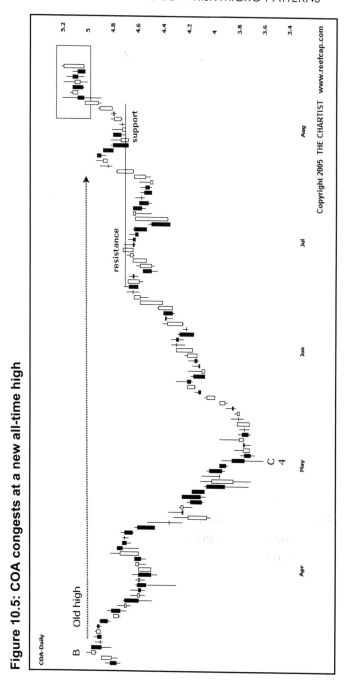

Figure 10.6: a micro box within a larger consolidation

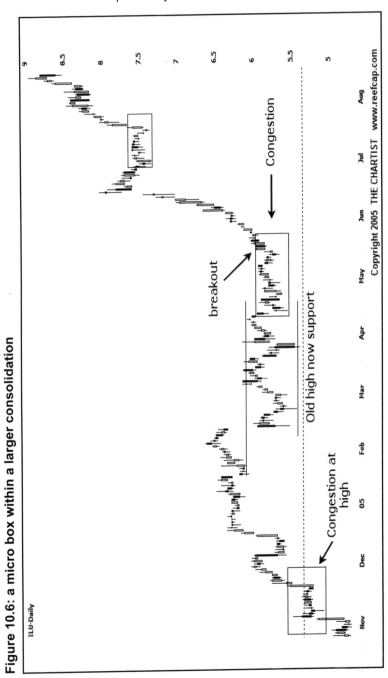

As shown in figure 10.7 overleaf, CBA broke into new highs in June 2005, just before a sideways congestion area was created. Prices broke out through the topside before consolidating yet again just above the old box. The old area of resistance became very good support, which provided the launch pad for all-time highs.

Using micro patterns to get in early

Apart from the low-risk advantages of micro patterns, another advantage is that not many people really look for them. Classical technicians are more interested in the larger and more obvious areas of support and resistance. The chart of Woolworths Ltd (WOW) in figure 10.8 on page 139 is an example of where a clear sideways range was breached in early February 2005. This breach turned out to be a false breakout and, while proper stop placement (at the line of resistance) would have enabled a trader to remain in for the move higher, his or her patience would have been tested and perhaps an early exit would have ensued. Also note the price range on the day where prices finally did breakout. Why was it such a large range? Probably because more classical chartists were watching for it and they all jumped on board at the same time.

Figure 10.7: sideways congestion just after new highs

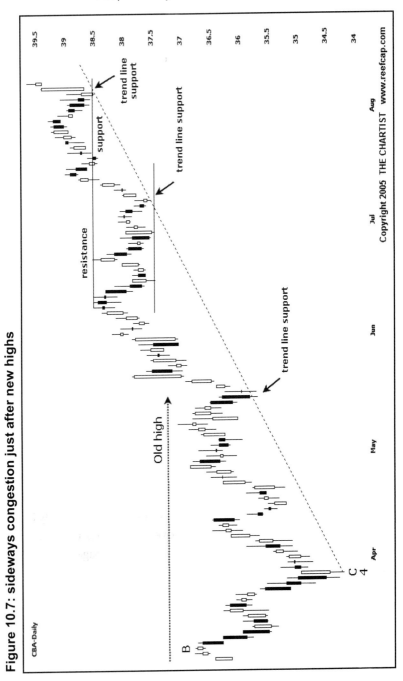

Interestingly enough, identifying the micro box within the major box (also shown in figure 10.8) would have allowed you to get the jump on the rest of the traders. They would have been concentrating on buying above the major box, not the minor one. Getting in first would have meant you could just ride on their coat-tails.

Figure 10.8: WOW showing contracting areas of consolidation

Consolidations in micro triangles

Figure 10.9 shows another very common pattern — the micro triangle. The major difference between a triangle and a box is that the triangle condenses into tighter ranges and decreasing volatility. This decreasing volatility tends to rapidly expand when prices finally break their shackles and, as such, a large move tends to ensue. As can be seen in figures 10.9, 10.10 and 10.11 (overleaf and page 142), points to note are, yet again, the triangles' sizes, their four internal points and that they occurred at an old high where buyers and sellers played tug of war until the trend finally resumed.

Adaptive Analysis for Australian Stocks

Figure 10.9: IAG and a micro triangle at an old high

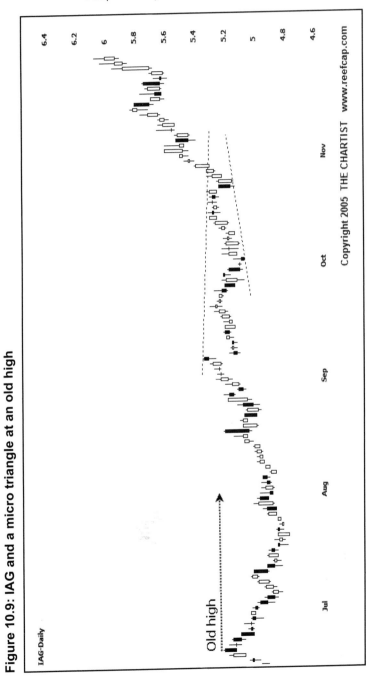

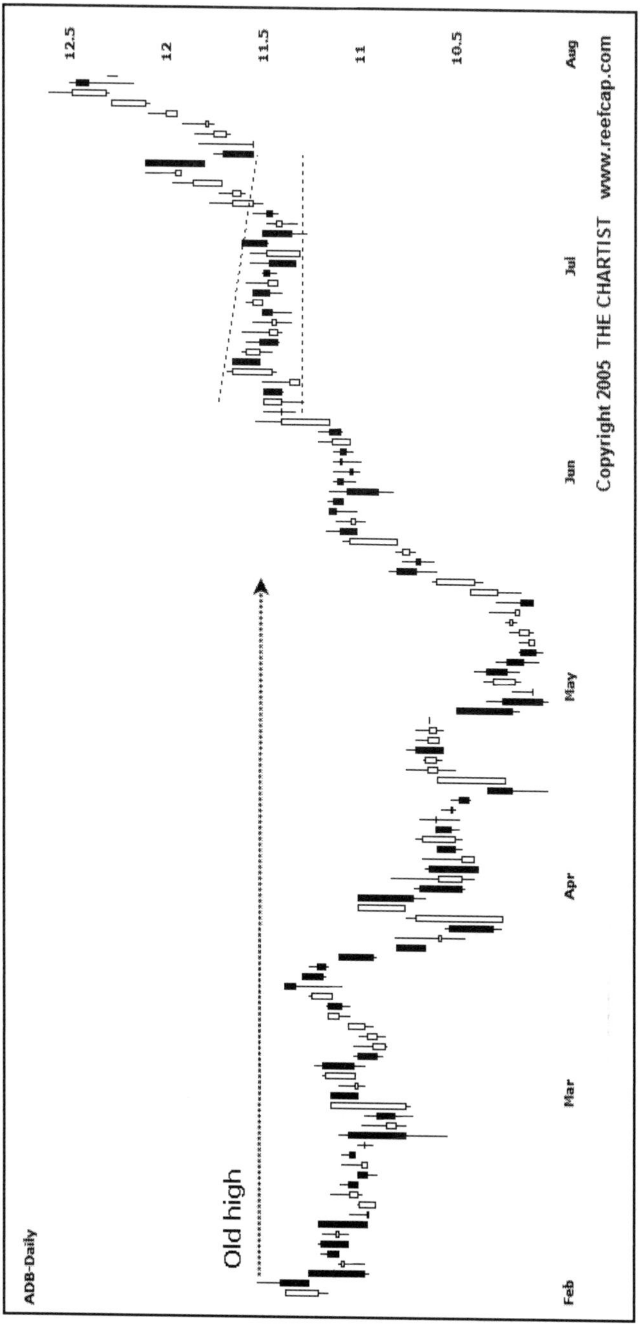
ADB-Daily
Old high
12.5
12
11.5
11
10.5
Feb
Mar
Apr
May
Jun
Jul
Aug
Copyright 2005 THE CHARTIST www.reefcap.com

Figure 10.10: ADB shows the continuation of trend through a micro triangle

Figure 10.11: PRK consolidates into a micro triangle

Figure 10.12 shows the distinct differences between a micro triangle and the more cited 'textbook' triangle. Textbook triangles are very large and can take months to form. The micro pattern occurs over a period from a number of days to a few weeks, and offers substantially less risk than its larger counterpart where the differences between entry and exit levels can be substantial.

Micro double bottoms and tops

Another powerful pattern is a micro double bottom within an uptrend or a micro double top within a downtrend. As you get experienced, you can trade these patterns *against* the trend; however, for now, let's play it safe and follow the line of least resistance. Like the other patterns, double tops and bottoms are extremely common and are largely overlooked by the majority of technicians. In this section, I will mainly discuss double bottoms — the rules are simply reversed for double tops. A double bottom occurs when two lows, punctuated by a number of days, stop at identical or almost identical levels. When they occur it suggests that buying support is present at that point and as such prices may move higher.

Figure 10.12: textbook and micro triangles

Copyright 2005 THE CHARTIST www.reefcap.com

Figure 10.13 (overleaf) shows the classic or textbook double top compared to the micro double bottom. The length of time between the two peaks that form the double-top pattern in the classic version is many months, whereas in the micro version it is a matter of days. Like the consolidation patterns, it all comes down to their size — the smaller they are, the lower the entry risk becomes.

Figure 10.13: a textbook double top versus a micro double bottom

The weekly chart of WOW in figure 10.14 shows further good examples of micro double bottoms within a sustained uptrend.

To use these patterns, you must define exactly what constitutes a double bottom because it is a rare occasion when both bottoms match each other to the cent. My interpretation of a double bottom is where two lows are a maximum of 0.5 per cent in price apart. The second point can be higher or lower than the first, but the low points must fall within 0.5 per cent of each other. Also part of the equation is the price action between the two lows, or the price pivot. There must be at least two bars (days or weeks) between each of the lows.

As can be seen in figure 10.15 on page 146, Alinta Ltd (ALN) had been a powerful trend for many months. The price action took a small breather, forming a double bottom, then the trend continued. In August 2005, prices exploded to new highs.

Figure 10.14: micro double bottoms within a strong uptrend

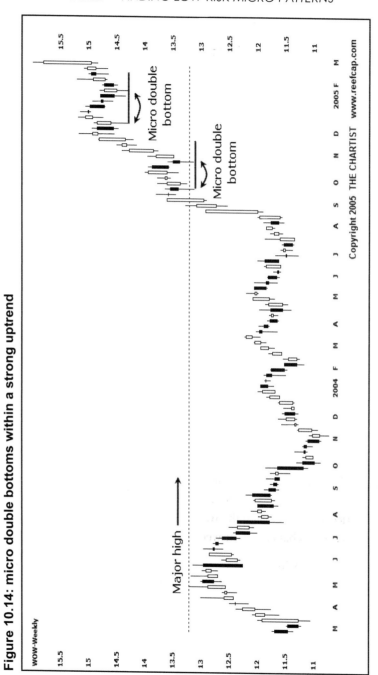

Adaptive Analysis for Australian Stocks

Figure 10.15: a double bottom within a strong uptrend

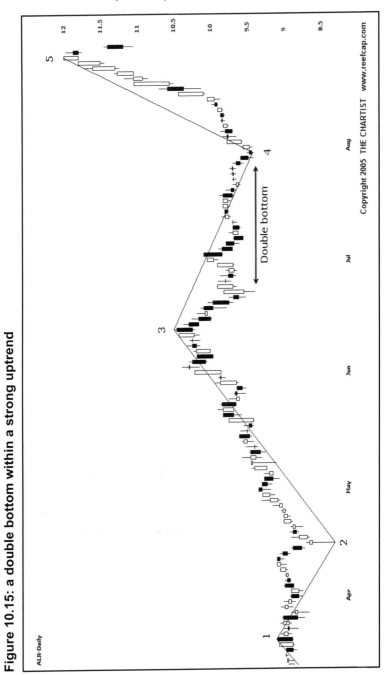

ALH-Daily

Copyright 2005 THE CHARTIST www.reefcap.com

Figure 10.16 shows micro double tops within a downtrend. Look at where the first double top occurred — exactly at the point of the gap, as prices filled the gap. This is an example of confluence (discussed earlier), as other indicators coincide with the pattern.

Figure 10.16: micro double tops within a downtrend

The same pattern can be seen on other time frames as well, such as within the weekly chart of Macmahon Holdings Ltd (MAH) shown in figure 10.17 overleaf. Like the price action of BLD shown in figure 10.16, there is also confluence here — in this case, it coincides with a multi-year trend line. Once again, this adds weight to its usefulness as a trading tool.

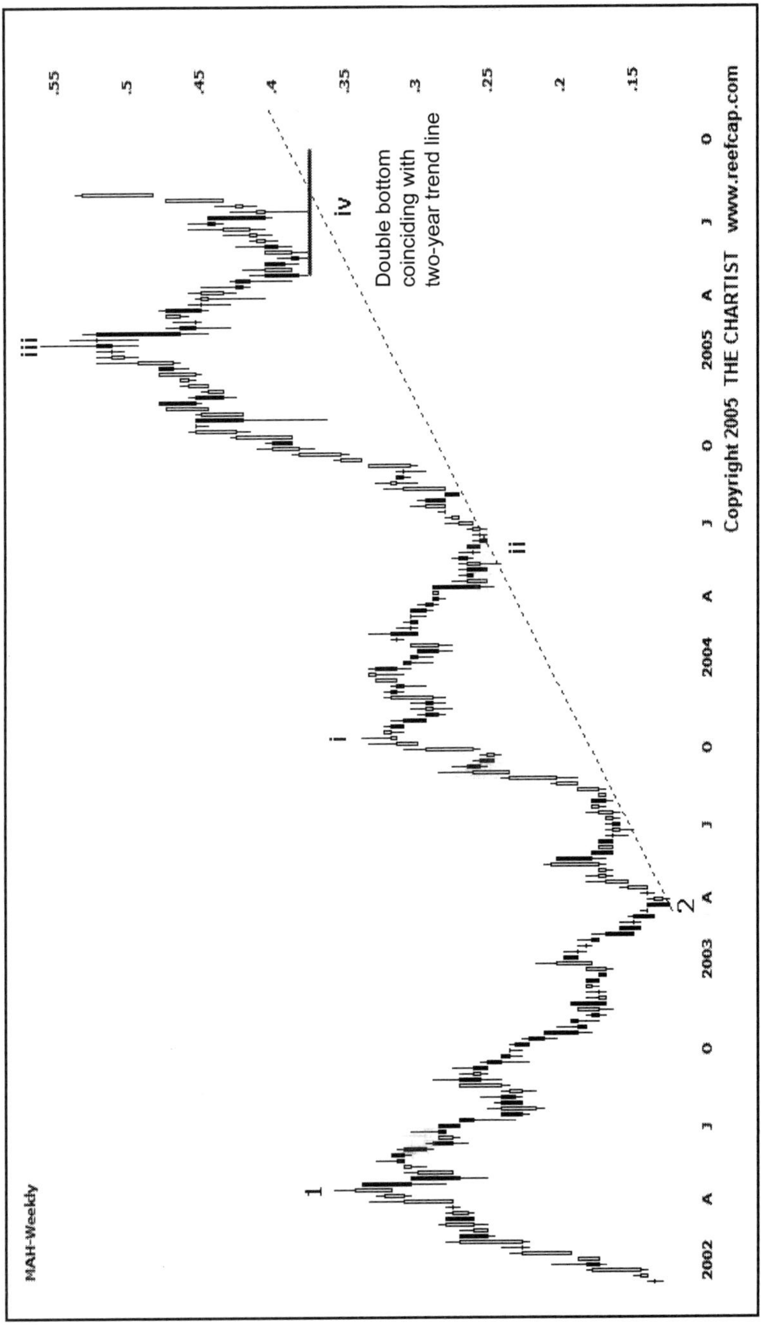

Adaptive Analysis for Australian Stocks

Figure 10.17: MAH shows a double-bottom formation coinciding with a multi-year trend line

MAH-Weekly

Double bottom
coinciding with
two-year trend line

Copyright 2005   THE CHARTIST   www.reefcap.com

Entering the market using micro patterns

The most likely question you wish to ask right now is, 'How do I use these patterns to enter the market?' Again, I will move away from the normal textbook examples and show you the method I have used since 1995, using the micro double-bottom pattern as an example.

As mentioned, the first criterion for the identification of a double-bottom pattern is that the two bottoms fall within the specified 0.5 per cent range of each other. The bar that makes the second low is counted as bar one. Counting backwards, you then need to find the most recent bar that made both a higher high and a higher low than bar one. All inside bars must be ignored. (An inside bar is one where the day's range does not exceed the prior day's range.)

The example in figure 10.18 shows the double bottom, marked 'Low #1' and 'Low #2'. The second low in the formation is marked '1'. The bar immediately before this has a higher high and a higher low, so it becomes bar two. This completes the set-up because the second low is 0.5 per cent from the first low and bar two meets the requirements of having a higher high and a higher low. How do we know that this will be the end of the double bottom and prices will start to rise? We don't. Prices may continue to fall, which will invalidate the pattern. If prices do start to rise, you enter the trade and prices then collapse again, you should have a protective stop in place to ensure you do not stay in the trade.

Figure 10.18: double-bottom set-up

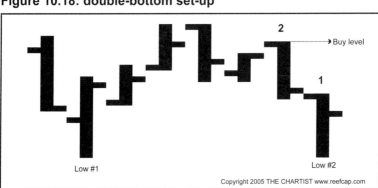

The high set by bar two is a trigger point to enter, so you would need prices to rise above this before you bought. Let's use an example. Say the high of bar two in the above example was $14.30. If, and only if, prices trade through $14.31, you would buy. You would not buy before prices reach that level. This is called a 'stop' entry — a buy stop would be placed above the market and would enable you to capture the momentum when and if prices start moving higher. You would not buy as prices were falling.

Figure 10.19 shows what could happen if prices moved through the buy level and continued higher.

Figure 10.19: a double bottom is successfully triggered

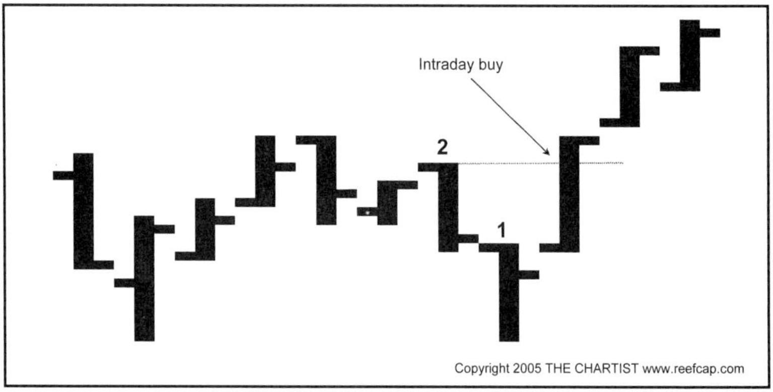

Once your buy level has been triggered and your broker has executed the buy order, you must place your protective stop just a few cents below the most recent low — in this example, below the second low. That is all you can control for now as the market will decide what happens next — either the trend will resolve itself or you will be stopped out.

Figure 10.20 of the price action of Westpac Banking Corporation (WBC) shows two double bottoms during a bullish trend. Count back from each second low to determine the entry point.

Figure 10.20: WBC showing multiple entry points

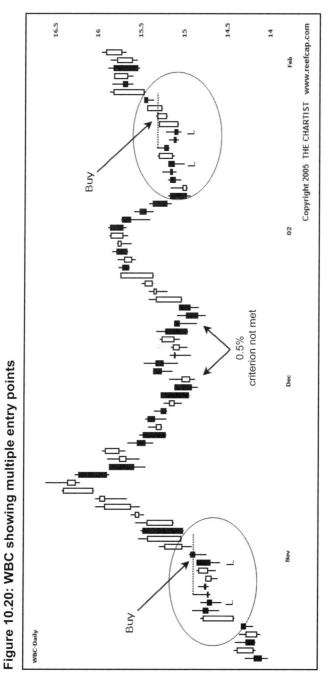

Not every trade will move immediately following the second low. CBA, in figure 10.21, showed a strong area of support that was able to hold prices above the protective stop level. This pattern became a triple bottom.

Figure 10.21: the double bottom acts as support after the entry

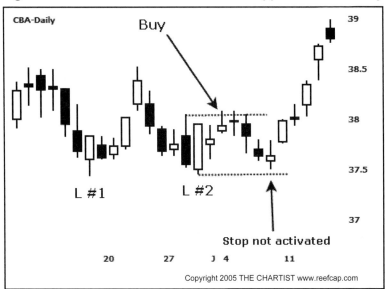

Figure 10.22 is exactly the same set-up except in reverse — meaning the set-up is for a short sell. The trend is down and there is a double top in place. Once you have counted back two bars from the second high, you know to sell on a breach of that bar's low. As can be seen in the chart, prices attempted to hold but slowly faded into a downtrend.

As can be seen in figure 10.23 on page 154, once the second low was made in Alinta, labelled as 'C' and '4', prices started moving up — rapidly activating a buy at $9.71 and allowing a very tight protective stop to be placed. In this case, the stop should be placed above the second high. This chart clearly identifies the potential risk/reward equation when these patterns form.

Figure 10.22: trading short off a double top

The same entry technique applies to all the micro patterns — simply look for a two-bar reversal off the low of the pattern when buying, or a two-bar reversal off the high when selling. Do they work all of the time? Of course not! Over the last 10 years, I've found that using these patterns to initiate low-risk entries has a success rate of around 50 per cent. In a bad year — 2001, for example — the win percentage dropped to 38 per cent. However, overall profits were still made. You may wish to further investigate other patterns or the possible use of certain indicators to help guide you through — but remember that an indicator is derived from price, so price should always be given the priority.

Figure 10.23: the potential risk/reward equation after a double bottom

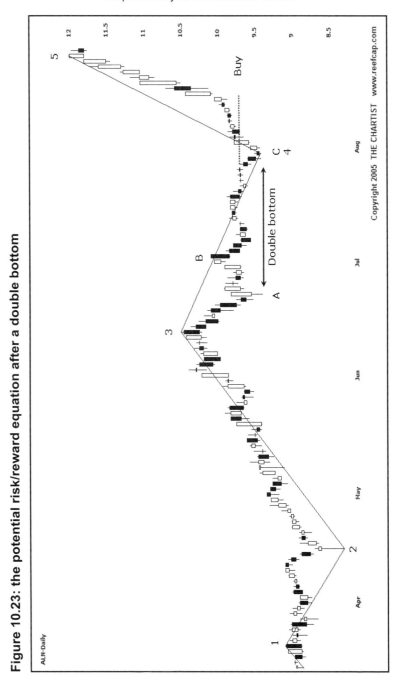

CHAPTER 11

THE ART
OF THE EXIT

Even after you've worked half your life to determine an appropriate entry mechanism, you will still be met with yet another incredibly frustrating element of trading — when to exit a trade. I can guarantee that many of you will never be at peace with your exits. You will always see yourself as getting out too early or too late and then beat yourself up about it. This is simply because the market is dynamic. It runs at different speeds at different times. Sometimes it runs very quickly while at other times it just drifts. There never seems to be a comfortable middle ground and the frustration can be unbearable for new traders. Unfortunately, I don't have the answers either — although I will give you a few insights that may help you along.

I have called this section 'the art of the exit' because it does require some skill, or at least modest powers of interpretation, to fully ride a position. Over the years I have developed a few methods, including the use of EW, that make me feel comfortable; however, you must find the way that makes *you* feel comfortable. Firstly, remember that to increase the risk/reward ratio you must try to ride the trend as far as possible. This becomes a balancing act between letting the trend run and not giving back too much open profit — and the balancing point will be different for each individual. I strive to allow the market room to move within its own daily variances. For example, if the market is swinging back and forth by $0.30 each day, I'll stay outside of that zone rather than have the position terminated due to general noise and not a proper correction.

Warning signs

Before getting into the actual mechanics of how I run my trailing stops, I will outline some of the analysis I use as 'warning signs' of a looming correction. These warning signs allow me to decide whether I exit the position completely, move the trailing stop up a little or move it up aggressively. Remember the EW guidelines discussed in chapter 5, specifically the following:

- Guideline two — wave two tends to retrace between 50 per cent and 70 per cent of wave one.

- Guideline three — wave four tends to retrace between 30 per cent and 50 per cent of wave three.

- Guideline four — wave one and wave five tend to be the same length.

Identifying the end of wave five

Let's start with guideline two and assume you've been riding a stock and you now notice that there are five distinct waves up. What you know is that when the end of this trend has occurred — that is, after the three-wave decline — the trend should form a new wave one, which in turn will be followed by a wave two. You also know that second waves tend to be deep, hence the importance of guideline two. In other words, if you suspect that the end of wave five is near, you certainly don't want to be hanging around too long. Take a look at the following chart of Tap Oil Ltd (TAP) in figure 11.1. According to my interpretation, the strong trend is certainly over.

Figure 11.1: TAP starts its major correction

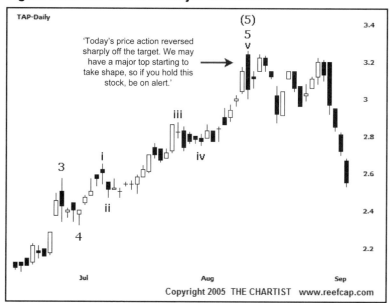

I am not one to suggest when an absolute high or low will be made. I use probabilities and sometimes they work and sometimes they don't. However, by using these probabilities I can better understand what may occur and adjust the stops accordingly — or at least get myself prepared to act quickly. On 3 August 2005, I suggested in my advisory service, The Chartist, that price could move through $3.00 and possibly hit $3.10. On 11 August, I made the following comment at the high on the chart, 'Today's price action sharply reversed off the target. We may have a major top starting to take shape, so if you hold this stock, be on alert'.

I was not saying that the top was an absolute high. I was saying that the probabilities were lining up that way and defensive action should be taken or at least thought about. Also, assuming that my analysis was correct up until that point and that all the fifth waves were occurring at that level, the expected sell off, according to guideline two, would be harsh. The best course of action would be to tighten the trailing stop so it was very, very tight, or just exit at the next available price.

When you are aware of the count, you can also be aware of how large the subsequent corrective move will be and therefore better gauge whether you should hold on and weather the correction, or just exit and wait for another opportunity. If you are aware of the guidelines, for example, you will usually be more inclined to weather a wave-four correction because they don't tend to be as harsh as wave-two declines.

But how do you decide on *where* the warning levels come into play? There is guideline four, which states wave five may terminate when it reaches the same length as wave one. However, I also use other measuring tools as well. While I did say that guidelines can become unnecessarily longwinded, there are just two more that I use. They are based on Fibonacci extensions.

Take another look at the TAP chart in figure 11.1. Notice the smaller wave count labelled as wave i through wave v.

Firstly, wave v equals wave i at $3.10, as per the basic fourth guideline.

Next, Fibonacci extensions can be used to set further targets. I learnt this technique back in 1995 when it was popularised by Robert Fischer in his book *Fibonacci Applications and Strategies for Traders* (John Wiley & Sons, 1993). Fischer suggested that the end of the fifth wave would tend to occur between two Fibonacci extension points. These extensions were:

1   1.618 × the length of wave one from the end of wave one

2   0.618 × the complete length of the start of wave one to the end of wave three from the end of wave three.

In the example above, the first wave in TAP started at $2.32 and ended at $2.65, which is a distance of $0.33. If this $0.33 is multiplied by 1.618 and then added to the $2.65, we arrive at a target of $3.18.

Using Fischer's second Fibonacci extension, the distance from the start of wave i to the end of wave iii was $0.55. If this $0.55 is multiplied by 0.618 and then added to the high of wave iii at $2.87, we arrive at $3.20.

There are now three separate measuring levels all pointing to the end of wave v somewhere between $3.10 and $3.20 — all shown in figure 11.2 (overleaf). The high was $3.26 and it coincided with a large reversal day. It isn't always as clean as this example, but I continue to be amazed at how often the levels correspond. Remember, though, you're only using these as evidence to prove the patterns you have identified, not as forecasting tools.

Identifying the end of wave three

But what about the end of wave three? Again, you can use two tools to allow you to get some type of idea of when this might occur. Firstly, wave three cannot be the shortest wave in the pattern. As such, the *minimum* length of wave three should be the same as the length of wave one. In the TAP example above, the length of wave i is $0.33. Therefore, wave iii must end at $2.80 ($2.47 + $0.33) or higher for the pattern to be confirmed. The second tool I use is also based on the concept of a Fibonacci extension and the 0.618 per cent ratio. I simply multiply the length of wave one by 0.618 and add it to the high of wave one. In this case, $0.33 × 0.618 = $0.20 and then $0.20 + $2.65 = $2.85. There is now some kind of indication that it is highly likely wave iii will end somewhere between $2.80 and $2.85. These points are marked on figure 11.3 (on page 161). It did in fact end at $2.87.

We can also measure the various wave lengths in the cycles of differing degrees to find more evidence. As mentioned, as a general rule of thumb, the smaller degree waves usually break down first, indicating that the larger degree waves may also be starting to fail. When you see these measured targets starting to cluster, you may decide to take defensive action. As it is likely a fourth wave will be a relatively shallow retracement, you may be more inclined to sit it through when it occurs.

Figure 11.2: confluence at a major high

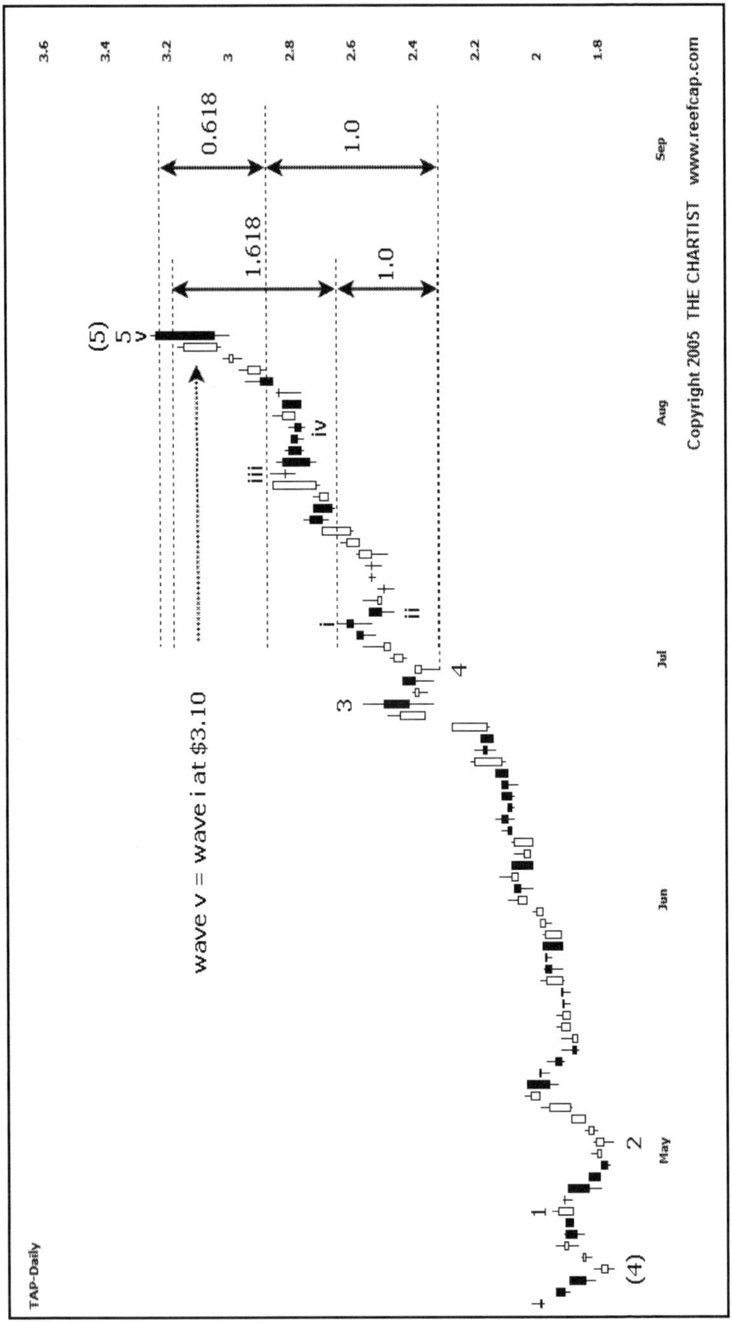

Figure 11.3: calculating the end of wave three

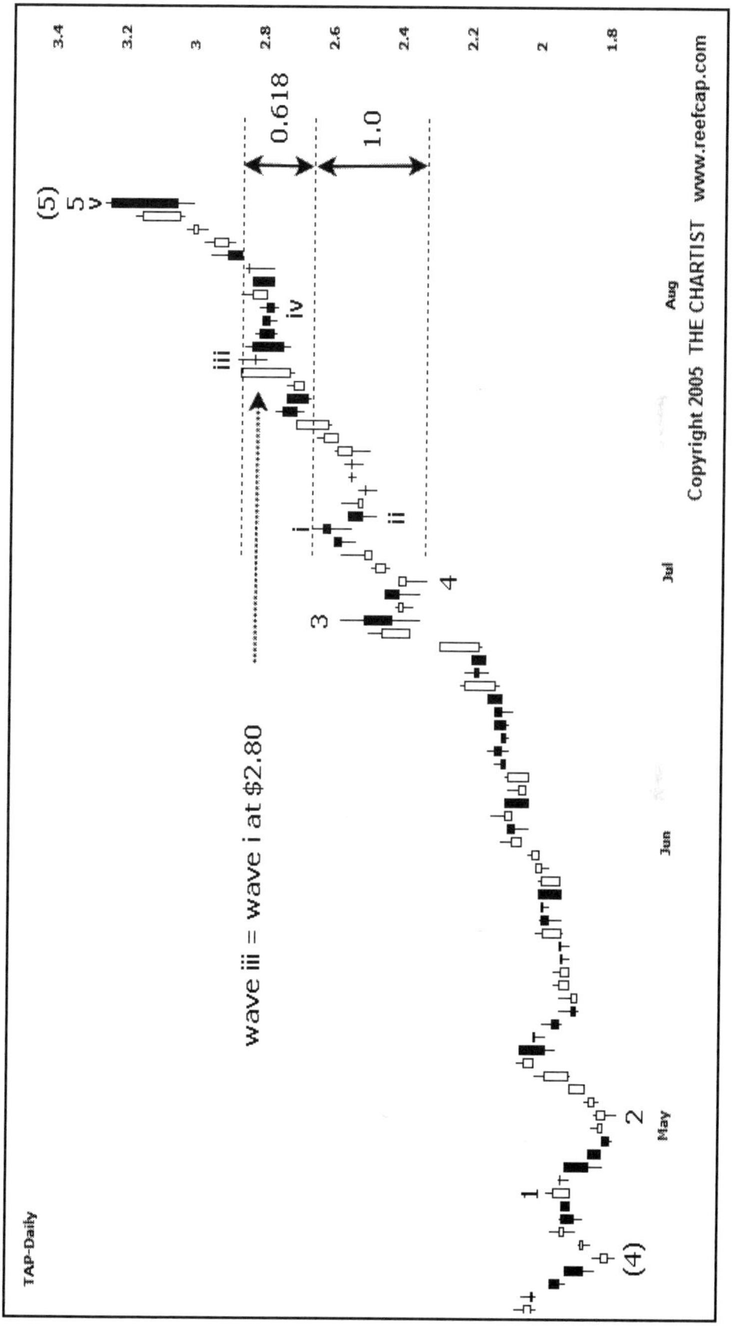

The speed of the market

As mentioned earlier, the market moves at different speeds at different times. The reasons behind this tend to be sentiment-based — for example, panic buying or selling usually causes faster prices, whereas no new information may create drifting prices. When a position is initiated under one condition and then the opposite condition makes its presence felt, the situation can be made even harder for traders. When this occurs it is imperative to adapt to the changing conditions, but always keep in mind that your primary job is to maximise the trend and not cut it short. To help with this, I really divide price action into two speeds — trending and accelerating.

Trending markets

Figure 11.4 shows Alinta forming a third wave at what I would define as trending speed. It was moving nicely, but was also showing small ebbs and flows along the way. One of the devices for determining the end of wave three is multiplying the length of wave one by 0.618 and adding this to wave one's high. As can be seen in figure 11.4, as prices started to approach the level identified by this device, they accelerated into it, which is a good sign. However, this example shows why you only use this as a warning, not an absolute point at which to exit the trade. After reaching the level, prices then returned to their pattern of ebb and flow. Because prices were now at the point of a *probable* end to the move, it was time to start being proactive with the protective stop to lock in the profits.

I use what I call a 'swing stop' — that is, whenever the market has a small swing down and then moves back up, I move the stop in below the low of that swing. You can see that I have noted three of these points on figure 11.4, marked as '1', '2' and '3'. Finally, at the third stop, prices fell below the low and the trade was stopped out. This method is by far the best way to follow a trend closely when a standard trend occurs, while also keeping you out of market noise when a sideways congestion area occurs.

Figure 11.4: ALN trending along

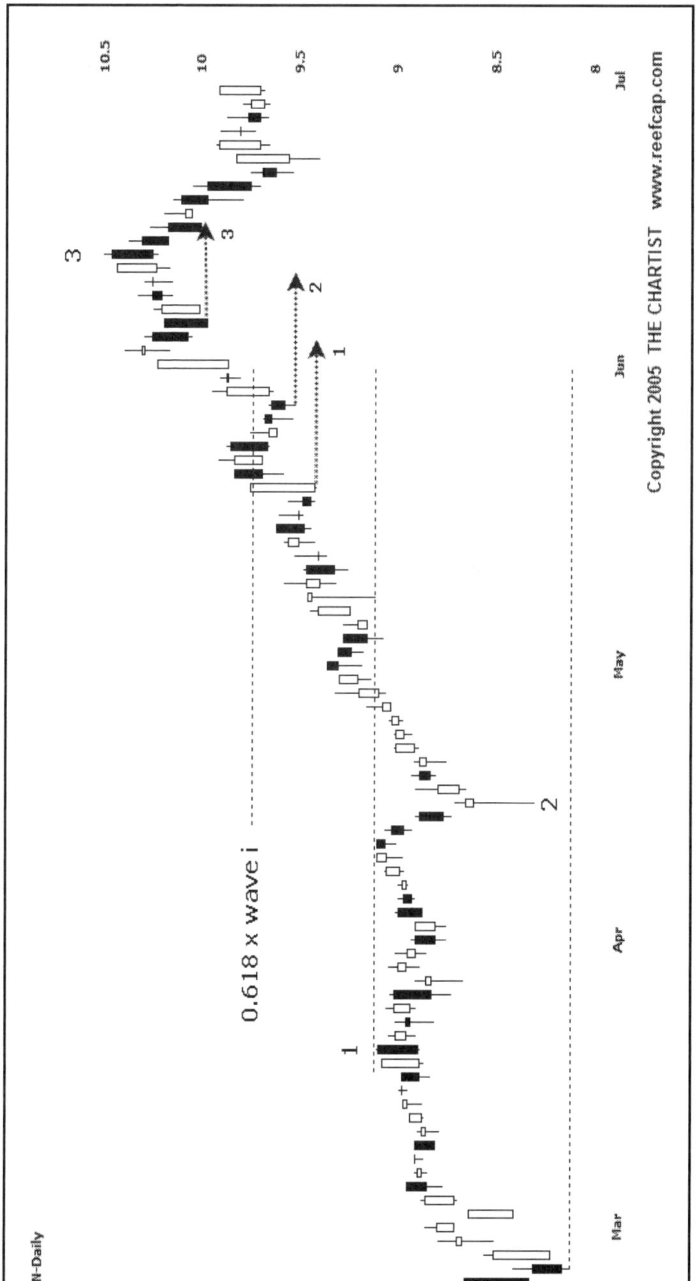

ALN-Daily

0.618 x wave i

Copyright 2005 THE CHARTIST www.reefcap.com

The recent rise and rise of Aristocrat Technologies Australia Pty Ltd (ALL), shown in figure 11.5, has been a good example of a 'stepping' trend — where the swing stop comes in very useful to keep you aligned with the ebb and flow.

Figure 11.5: ALL swinging along

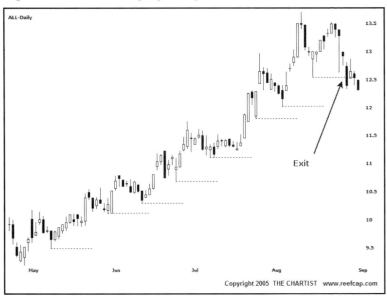

Accelerating markets

The chart of Seven Network Ltd (SEV) in figure 11.6 shows a typical sequence of events. The price was trending nicely higher, doing its usual ebb and flow before moving into a period of consolidation. The swing levels have been marked and you can see that they allowed me to stay with the trend, even through the consolidation phase, until the market broke upward and started accelerating. Patience is needed, but that is often the nature of stock prices — a lot of ebb and flow punctuated by areas of congestion and acceleration.

Figure 11.6: three phases of stock price movement — trend, congestion and acceleration

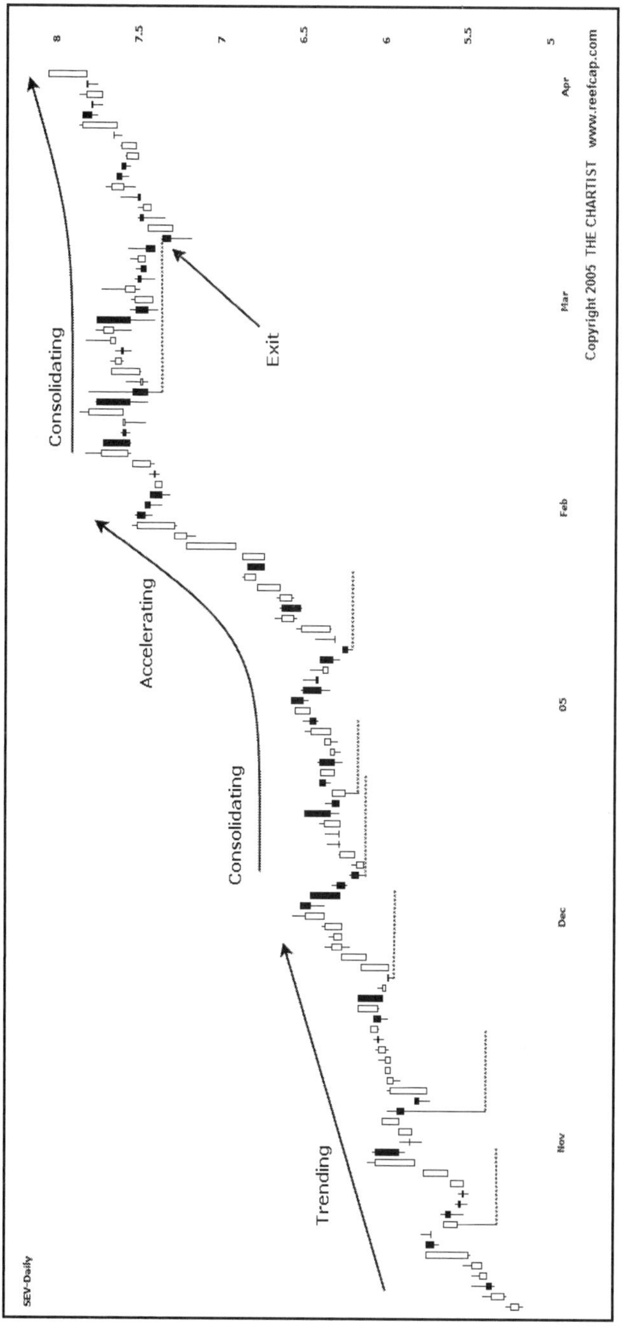

SEV-Daily

Trending

Consolidating

Accelerating

Consolidating

Exit

Nov   Dec   05   Feb   Mar   Apr

8   7.5   7   6.5   6   5.5   5

Copyright 2005 THE CHARTIST   www.reefcap.com

As you can see, accelerating price action gets that parabolic look to it. An accelerating market is always the most exciting, but it can also be the most heart-wrenching for the new trader. A beginner is usually more concerned that the price will reverse sharply and will want to take the profit. Again, you can just never know what prices will do. The market will do what it wishes and you can only manage your feelings accordingly.

Figure 11.7 shows Alinta accelerating into a fifth wave. Not only did it have eight straight days of higher highs and higher lows, the actual size, or price ranges, on those days also increased.

Figure 11.7: ALN accelerates into a trend before faltering

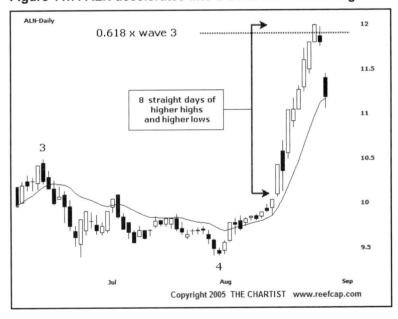

When a stock or market starts accelerating, the swing stop discussed above is not particularly efficient — simply because there can be a long distance between the swings. As a result, I change my tack and apply an exponential moving average (EMA) to the chart. When that EMA is breached *intraday*, I'm out. I use 13 days for the EMA; however, you should choose a length that suits you. Just remember, though — the lower the number of days, the tighter the stop. Again, it's a balancing act. I have used 13 for many years — unfortunately, there is no fancy reason why; it just suits me.

While ALN appeared to be a very strong stock, the trend did end abruptly. This type of ending, where the price action forms a deep 'V', tends to cause the most frustration for traders — usually because they already had their profits counted in their minds. Although the Fibonacci extension did provide a clue to where wave five could end, the day you attempt to predict the specific top is the day the price really shoots higher. And let me tell you from experience — nothing hurts more than missing a great trade.

Monitoring your exits (and entries)

If you are genuinely concerned and really frustrated about your exits, you can take steps to monitor their efficiency and pick up information that can help in managing them better.

You can use the following simple formulae on winning trades to check your efficiency. (There is not much you can do for a losing trade.) The various efficiency measures are:

- **Entry efficiency = (High − Entry) ÷ (High − Low)**
  (should be greater than 60 per cent)
- **Exit efficiency = (Exit − Low) ÷ (High − Low)**
  (should be greater than 60 per cent)
- **Total efficiency = (Exit − Entry Price) ÷ (High − Low)**
  (should be greater than 40 per cent).

To explain how the concept works, let's assume that ABC Pty Ltd starts its trend up at zero and hits a high of 10 before moving lower again. Say your method allows you to enter at two and your protective stop is hit at seven. The net profit of your trade is five (seven minus two), which is 50 per cent (five divided by 10) of the total trend. The trade efficiency for the complete move is therefore 50 per cent, which is a good result. Ideally, when you trade a trend you should aim to capture the 'meat' or the middle of the move, and a 40 per cent or higher capture is good.

Taking this basic concept a little further, you can also determine if the entry and/or exits are hindering your performance. Again, using the same scenario, you were able to enter the trade at two, meaning from the entry to the end of the trend you could potentially have caught 80 per cent (eight divided by 10). The exit efficiency in the example was 70 per cent, because you exited seven points above the low and three points below the high. Both of these figures are also good, as the entry and exit efficiencies should both be above 60 per cent. Hence, if you achieve these levels, you have done quite well and you should be happy.

If you see a pattern start to form in your trading whereby your exit efficiency is very low, you need to ask yourself why. Is the stop too loose? Are you selecting stocks that are too volatile or do not trend enough? Conversely, if the exit efficiency is too high, you may also have a problem when you think it through. Why would you have an extremely high exit efficiency? Most likely because your stop is too tight. If you see this occurring, you should measure your efficiency using the high two weeks *after* you exited. By using a high that occurred after you have exited, you may start to see that the trend continued without you on board.

If you find that your entry efficiency is low, you may need to look at your entry technique. It may be that you are waiting for too many indicators to align themselves or for too much price confirmation before entering. Whatever the reason, the bottom line is that you're slow to enter and that is costing you a valuable part of the trend.

Trading records

While we're on the subject of efficiency scores and discussing their value, it is also worthwhile discussing the importance of keeping accurate trading records. This will allow you to look honestly at your trading and pinpoint areas that can be improved. It also allows you to trade your capital more (or less) aggressively through understanding the nuances that appear within the data.

Examine table 11.1, which shows a simplified record of the wins and losses of two traders. Both appear to be the same — in particular, both appear to set their risk at $250 per trade. What would concern me is why Trader Two had a $900 loss at trade number 15 when his average loss to that point was less than $250? Did he forget to place his protective stop? Was it simply an unfortunate event? (And yes, they do occur.) Or was it something more sinister, such as deciding he was right on the trade and refusing to acknowledge he was wrong, and so he allowed himself to keep moving his protective stop?

Table 11.1: wins and losses of two traders

Trade number	Trader One		Trader Two	
	Win	Loss	Win	Loss
1		120		250
2	415		500	
3	280		900	
4	960		960	
5		250		250
6	180		400	
7		175		175
8		192		192
9	300		30	
10	400		250	
11		250		250
12		250		250
13	500		500	
14	400		650	
15		250		900
16	630		400	

If, for example, Trader Two was simply unlucky on trade 15 because of a poor fill or excess slippage (slippage is the difference between where you wanted your trade to be filled and where it actually was filled in the market), he has nothing to be concerned about. However, if his loss occurred because he didn't concede he was wrong and so adjusted his stop on a few occasions, he must address that flaw because the day will come when he will do some very serious damage to his account. Indeed, if this type of event occurs on a regular basis, he should be concerned for his future as a trader and seek help.

However, if he was disciplined and never adjusted his stop but continually had excess slippage that made losses such as trade 15 reasonably common, Trader Two could still have a problem. To me, it would possibly indicate that the markets he was trading in were too thin. If it happened too often, he should move to more liquid markets because his trades are costing him money. The lack of liquidity will also stop him trading larger trades or pyramiding his trades if he does get to that point. The lower the liquidity of the market, the less volume it can absorb and therefore the higher the slippage factor will become.

Trade monitoring is essential in running your business of trading. Keep accurate records and continually ask yourself the hard questions about your performance.

BRINGING IT
ALL TOGETHER

In parts I and II, I outlined the philosophies that I trade by as well as the steps I use to help myself feel comfortable enough to initiate a position and risk money in the market. These factors, plus experience, form my trading plan. In part III, I would like to bring all these pieces together using examples current at the time of writing, just to show that you don't need to look too far to find opportunities around you, and also to outline the impact the factors have when combined.

The pieces required to determine your trading plan are:

- clarifying your overall philosophy on profitability, risk management and trade management
- defining the trend
- finding areas of confluence for a potential entry
- identifying a low-risk entry pattern.

I'll now go through the price action on various stocks to show you my exact thinking at specific times and why I considered a trade or stood aside.

CHAPTER 12

AUSTRALIAN STOCK EXCHANGE LTD (ASX)

8 July 2005

Prices had risen from just above $19.00 in April 2005 as part of the beginning of a larger wave five, shown in figure 12.1. This rise formed a smaller five-wave pattern, labelled 'i', 'ii', 'iii', 'iv' and 'v', which culminated at $23.48 on 10 June. This peak, labelled as a new wave-1 high, was confirmed by a substantial sell off that in turn suggested wave two was under way. I felt a buy opportunity would soon present itself within the larger bullish picture.

Over the following month, prices formed a low at $22.29 and then again at $22.15. Two issues bothered me here. Firstly, the set-up was not quite a double bottom by my definition, because the lows just missed being within 0.5 per cent of each other. Secondly, the wave-two retracement was very shallow. I am always cautious of a shallow correction in this phase because it may be a sign that the price action is simply part of a larger corrective move yet to come. At this point, I chose to stand aside and let prices resolve themselves into a clearer opportunity.

Figure 12.1: ASX, 8 July 2005

19 July 2005

Over the next week, prices pushed outside of the range and peaked again at $23.96, as shown in figure 12.2. In the face of a very strong, broader market, I started to think a deeper retracement for wave two may not eventuate. A breakout of a range followed by a small pullback is a very common occurrence before prices go higher, and here it was presented yet again. I felt that if prices moved up from here, wave two would be confirmed and a push into wave three would be under way. The length of wave one was $4.27, so the length of wave three must be at least that distance. This suggested prices could rise to $26.42 if my analysis was correct. An entry on a breakout from $23.96 would allow a stop to be placed at the low of that retest ($23.32), equalling a risk of $0.64. If $26.42 was to be seen, the potential profit would be $2.46 or a risk/reward of 3.8, which is acceptable.

Figure 12.2: ASX, 19 July 2005

28 July 2005

Over the following week, prices did rally but fell short of the $26.42 level when the company announced its profit results and prices gapped sharply lower, as shown in figure 12.3. The problem was that the high had been just $26.20, meaning the wave three I had been looking for had not completed or my analysis was incorrect. Remember that wave three needed to achieve a minimum of $26.42 to be valid. Looking closer at the chart, I realised a new pattern was emerging within the larger wave three. I have labelled that smaller pattern with 'i', 'ii' and 'iii'. If this pattern held together, wave v could take prices through to the $26.42 level and complete the larger wave three that I had been looking for. In other words, this sharp reversal after the profit results was possibly wave iv. Interestingly enough, after the reversal, most brokers downgraded the stock and suggested that it should return to $20.00.

Figure 12.3: ASX, 28 July 2005

17 August 2005

As at the time of writing, prices have consolidated and created a wave iv that still remains within the larger wave three that I have been trading. As shown in figure 12.4, a new high at $26.35 has been hit since the profit announcement, but this still fell just short of the $26.42 minimum I require. Clearly, if the low of the minor wave iv at $25.21 is broken before the $26.42 level is hit, I remain incorrect with the analysis and it will be time to exit the position. Hence, my protective stop has been placed at $25.21.

Figure 12.4: ASX, 17 August 2005

CHAPTER 13

ONESTEEL LTD (OST)

June 2005

OST got my interest in June 2005 when a weekly downtrend was broken by a powerful thrust, as shown as figure 13.1. Further inspection of the chart also showed a zigzag pattern, labelled 'A', 'B', 'C', from the high at $3.20 down to the low at $2.20. While I hadn't noticed any predominant wave count up until that point, such a zigzag or three-wave overlapping pattern suggested a corrective move. Therefore, I began to think that the low at $2.20 was possibly a major low and that some type of buy entry might shortly emerge.

Figure 13.1: OST, June 2005

19 July 2005

After the trend line break, prices settled back to retest that line — a very common occurrence. This retest is shown in figure 13.2, a daily chart of the price action. I saw the minor peak at $2.77 as a small wave-three high, meaning this retest could become a wave-four correction. Remember that wave fours tend to be shallow and flat or triangular in nature. This was no exception — as the old resistance became new support, a descending triangle formed. This support held on three occasions, which told me any move higher may well have a strong follow-through as wave five. The buy level was set at $2.64 and a tight protective stop could therefore be placed below the support area at $2.57. The risk on this trade was $0.07 with a probable target of $2.90 (the point at which wave five equals the length of wave one), representing a $0.26 profit or a risk/reward ratio of 3.7.

Figure 13.2: OST, 19 July 2005

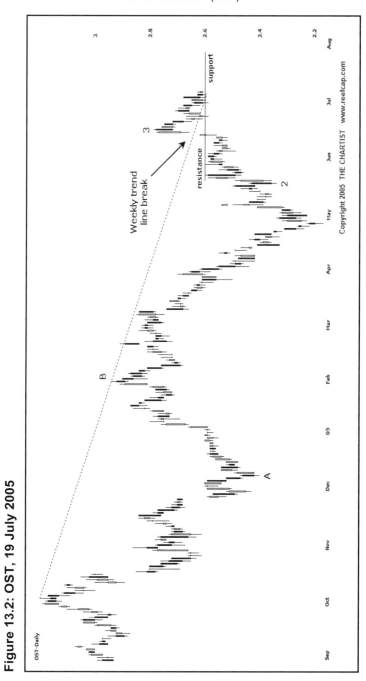

ONE STEEL LTD (OST)

181

28 July 2005

Prices pushed to test the wave-three high and just breached them before retreating, as shown in figure 13.3. I am always ready for some consolidation at old highs but considering I was only looking for $2.90, I didn't want to have the trade turn into a loss. When prices started retreating, I moved my protective stop up to below the lows made at $2.68 a few days prior. Unfortunately, a small spike down was enough to take me out of the trade. I still saw this as a wave-four correction and was ready to wait for another opportunity to come along.

Figure 13.3: OST, July 28 2005

17 August 2005

Not much need be said here, except that I failed to re-enter because my attention was elsewhere and I had not expected this price action to unfold. After the current strength to new highs and considering the major break of the trend line, as shown in figure 13.4, the termination of wave five will signal the start of a new pattern, so I'll be on the lookout for a new wave (2) to trade.

Figure 13.4: OST, 17 August 2005

CHAPTER 14

AUSTRALIAN WORLD-WIDE EXPLORATIONS LTD (AWE)

20 May 2005

AWE attracted my interest when prices fell from a major high at $2.14 to $1.50, as shown in figure 14.1. It did so in a three-wave, A-B-C formation (not shown in the chart). Some confluence was also at play. Firstly, wave C and wave A were almost equal lengths. The low at wave (C) also coincided with the 0.382 per cent retracement level of the multi-year rally that started at $0.75 in early 2003. Prices rejected this area convincingly, creating a pattern known as a 'blow-off' bottom. A quick move to $2.00 ensued before prices drifted toward $1.60. This appeared to be a large first and second wave forming. Another very small bounce occurred followed by a third retest of the 0.382 per cent level. If the low, identified as wave two, held, I had a very low-risk entry level for what potentially could be a large move to new highs within a third wave.

Figure 14.1: AWE, 20 May 2005

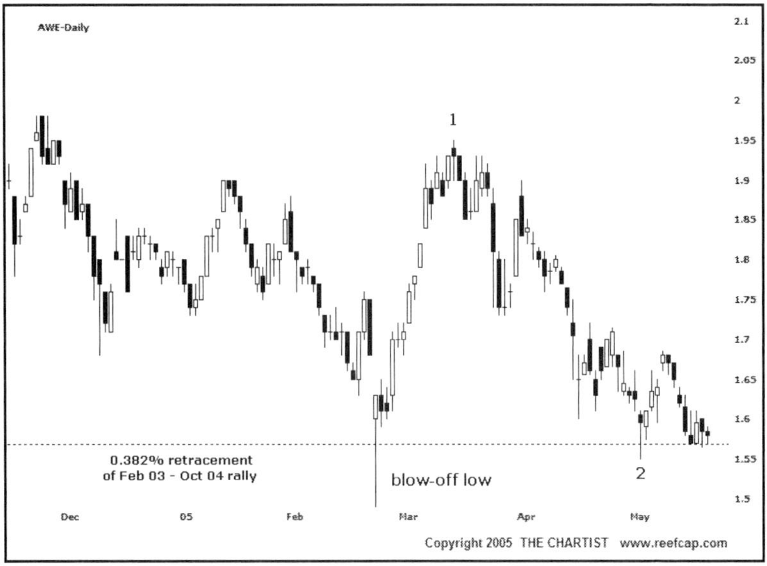
AWE-Daily
2.1
2.05
2
1.95
1.9
1.85
1.8
1.75
1.7
1.65
1.6
1.55
1.5
1
0.382% retracement
of Feb 03 - Oct 04 rally
blow-off low
2
Dec
05
Feb
Mar
Apr
May
Copyright 2005 THE CHARTIST www.reefcap.com

22 June 2005

As can be seen in figure 14.2, the expected price action certainly did occur — mainly with the help of the price of oil, which was in the process of scaling dazzling new heights. Prices pushed through to new highs without any degree of difficulty and this confirmed that the trend was certainly strong. A reasonably sharp sell off suggested that the minor wave iii was completed and that wave iv should start to take shape. Being near the high identified as wave one, I expected a sideways or triangular congestion to occur, most likely supported by that high.

Figure 14.2: AWE, 22 June 2005

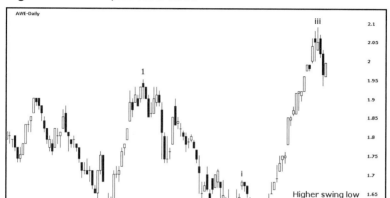

18 July 2005

The sideways price action was moving along just fine until the micro box failed and prices drifted to the downside, as shown in figure 14.3. While this certainly did not invalidate the analysis or trend, a deep fourth wave suggests to me that the following fifth wave may well be short. In this case, I thought wave v would just test the recent highs at around $2.10 to $2.15. Because of this lack of follow-through and the minimal potential risk/reward I had calculated, I chose to stand aside.

Figure 14.3: AWE, 18 July 2005

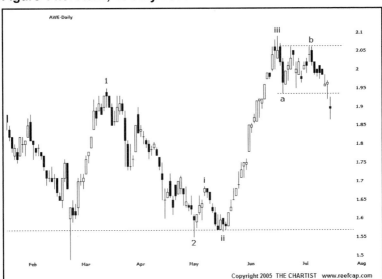

19 August 2005

Prices surged a lot more than I anticipated and left me waiting at the bus stop, as shown in figure 14.4. The major decline and gapping price action on 18 August suggests that wave v and the larger wave three have now been completed and I am now looking for the larger wave four. The wave-iii high should act as support and this connects with the trend line. Wave four would also be 0.382 per cent of wave three at this level, so some nice confluence is occurring. This wave four should take a week or two to resolve itself and will hopefully allow me a bigger ride on the coat-tails of the larger wave five.

Figure 14.4: AWE, 19 August 2005

CHAPTER 15

PATRICK CORPORATION LTD (PRK)

November 2004

PRK appeared on my radar screen in late 2004 when it broke to new highs at the $6.00 level, as shown in figure 15.1. I always find new highs as a good starting point to get a possible count going, especially on a larger time frame, before reverting to a smaller time frame for the actual trading. Also of interest was the large double bottom formed from April 2002 to April 2003, which laid the foundation for a possible new wave count.

January 2005

Over December 2004, prices kept pushing into new high territory; however, in early January 2005, signs of slowing momentum started to show. Prices pushed higher and then fell, closing below the opening price for the week, as shown in figure 15.2. This was weak price action and suggested a possible top if further downside momentum followed. Over the next week, prices dropped quite substantially, confirming that the old $6.00 breakout level was being tested. If this was the start of a new wave (2), I needed to see prices a lot lower than $6.00 before committing. A 0.50 per cent retracement came in at $5.21, aligned with the smaller degree third-wave high. A 0.618 per cent retracement came in at $4.81, which also aligned with the smaller degree fourth-wave low. To me, this area of confluence formed an area where a bullish position could be initiated.

Figure 15.1: PRK, November 2004

Figure 15.2: PRK, January 2005

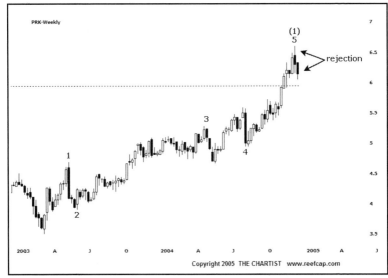

23 June 2005

As can be seen in figure 15.3, on May 18 PRK hit $5.16 and formed a perfect double bottom. The 0.50 per cent retracement level was at $5.21, so confluence and the low-risk pattern both existed. It was a ripe opportunity to initiate a longer term position; however, I had been a little greedy and had entered already on the way down at $5.71.

Prices pushed off this low back toward the $6.00 level yet again. It seemed that $6.00 was some type of pivotal area where price gyrated. This area played an important role because it also coincided with a minor downtrend line and this was enough to deter further buying strength. Prices sold off from here and I marked that trend line test as a new wave one within the much larger wave (3) that was under way.

Figure 15.3: PRK, 23 June 2005

27 July 2005

As can be seen in figure 15.4 on page 195, the minor second wave retraced almost exactly 0.618 per cent of the first wave. However, there were two problems hanging over prices as far as I was concerned — firstly, there was no discernible low-risk pattern that coincided with the wave-two low; secondly, the trend line bothered me as I felt it was still influencing more traditional analysts. I really wanted to see that breached first before being comfortable about entering. I wasn't concerned about trying to get the absolute lowest price because the larger wave (3) showed plenty of upside potential, so missing $0.50 wasn't an issue in this trade.

The solid thrust through the trend line in late July gave me hope that it had finally been overcome. It was now just a matter of finding a low-risk entry — hopefully on the top side of that line.

5 August 2005

The price action on 5 August 2005 certainly looked positive. As figure 15.5 on page 196 shows, a very minor double bottom had formed and, more importantly, it had formed above the trend line during a very bullish day. I decided that any follow-through to the upside would be as good a place as any to enter — a breach of $5.96 would allow such an entry, and a tight stop could then be placed just below the double bottom.

19 August 2005

Over the next two weeks, prices got a bit choppy and eventually got the better of me, as shown in figure 15.6 on page 197. This is always a problem when a tight stop is used — but because I will always find another opportunity to enter, it is something I have learnt to deal with. Clearly, in this case the analysis was correct and remains correct as far as the wave count goes. I can find comfort in knowing that the trend is firmly up and look for another entry level.

Figure 15.4: PRK, 27 July 2005

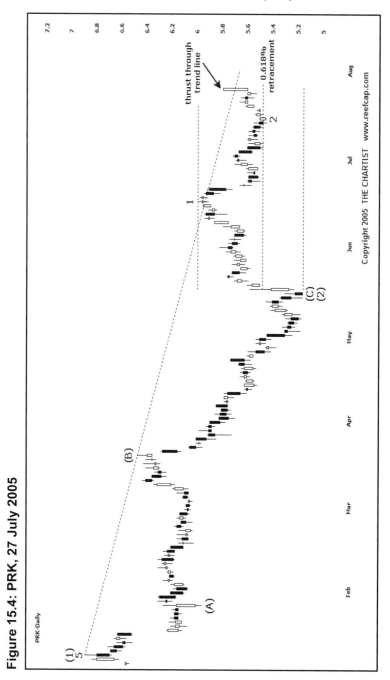

PATRICK CORPORATION LTD (PRK)

195

Figure 15.5: PRK, 5 August 2005

Adaptive Analysis for Australian Stocks

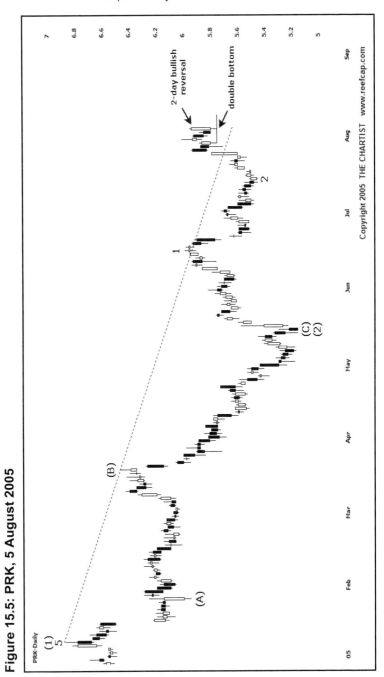

Copyright 2005 THE CHARTIST www.reefcap.com

196

Figure 15.6: PRK, 19 August 2005

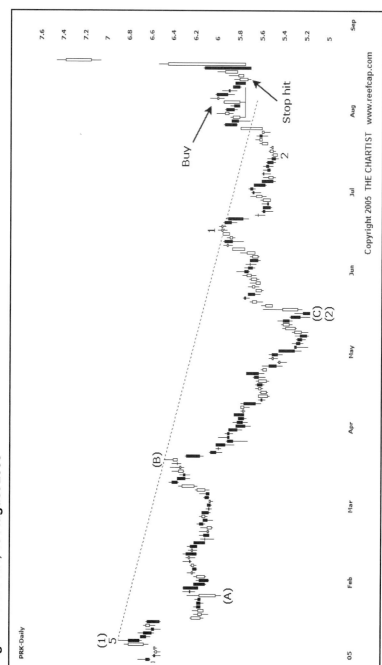

PATRICK CORPORATION LTD (PRK)

PRK-Daily

Copyright 2005   THE CHARTIST   www.reefcap.com

197

PART IV
CHARTING
THE FUTURE

Rarely does a book not rely on well-chosen examples. I decided to stray from the standard of using historical examples and base this last part on some of my thoughts on the future prospects of various stocks, using technical analysis and more specifically Elliott wave (EW) theory. At the time of writing, there are hundreds of examples, on both short-term and long-term charts, where EW can be successfully applied. My selection here is simply random.

My analysis was performed in mid-August 2005. Please take the time to re-read the disclaimer on page v before proceeding. The stocks are intended as examples only, and the views and analysis expressed herein were appropriate at the time of writing, but may change in the future.

CHAPTER 16

ADELAIDE BANK LTD (ADB)

Since ADB listed, the price action has shown perfect ebb and flow, allowing well-defined wave counts to be considered, as shown in figure 16.1. The current trend remains bullish, with what appears to be a subdividing of the larger wave five into a smaller pattern. That smaller pattern is known as an 'extension' and is typical in stock prices during the last wave. The risk to this current interpretation is actually to the upside, where the extension may be part of wave three and not wave five as I'm currently seeing it. Because the extension is more common in the fifth wave, I'll retain my reading; however, it may need to be reassessed in due course. The danger areas, where the smaller waves start to break down and become invalidated, are a long way off from current prices.

Figure 16.1: Adelaide Bank Ltd (ADB)

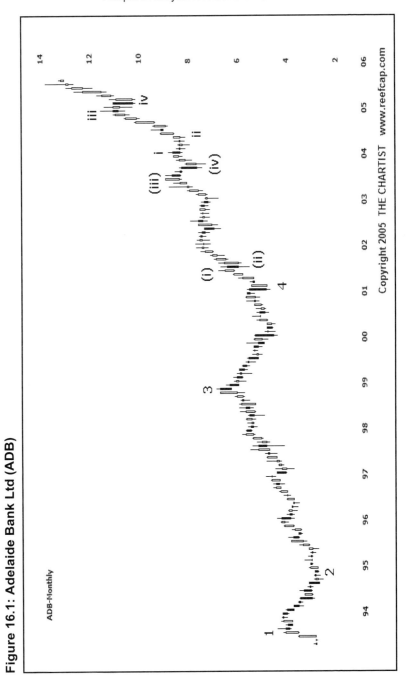

ADB-Monthly

CHAPTER 17

ANZ BANKING GROUP LTD (ANZ)

At the time of writing, the outlook for ANZ remains bullish, albeit with a hint of caution. It wasn't until 1996 that prices were able to break through a 10-year trading range that was capped at $6.00. As shown in the monthly chart in figure 17.1, the subsequent rise has followed the rules of EW very nicely and my interpretation that the major wave five is forming after prices moved out of a triangle that represented the wave-four correction. Early guidance from this chart suggests that prices may falter around $22.00, as it represents a minor confluence of Fibonacci levels and price measurements. However, better guidance for the immediate future of prices must be collected from the daily charts. These show a slightly more disturbing picture.

From February 2005 through to August 2005, prices were rejecting the $22.00 to $22.38 zone on a number of occasions. For the trend to continue, this barrier must be overcome. If this zone cannot be overcome, the first sign of trouble will be if $21.00 is breached to the downside, as this may signal a further decline back into the larger sideways area previously defined by the triangle (also shown in figure 17.1).

Figure 17.1: ANZ Banking Group Ltd (ANZ)

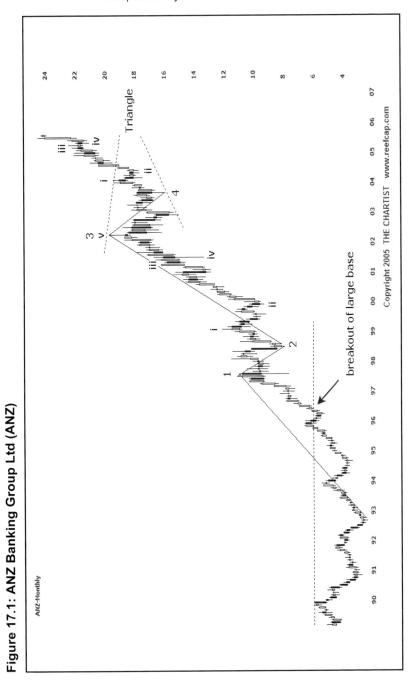

CHAPTER 18

AMP LTD (AMP)

Unfortunately, unless $9.42 can be broken in its price action, I cannot get overly excited about the long-term prospects of AMP — unlike many fundamental analysts. As can be clearly seen in figure 18.1, the stock has formed an impulsive move downward from 2001 to 2003. What I see in more recent times is really no different to what was seen from late 1999 to 2001 — that is, simply a bounce in an ongoing downtrend. If $9.42 can be broken, my analysis is clearly wrong because one of the core EW rules will have been broken. The interim picture suggests that while some short-term strength is possible, in terms of the very broad range over the coming years, the trend is down.

Figure 18.1: AMP Ltd (AMP)

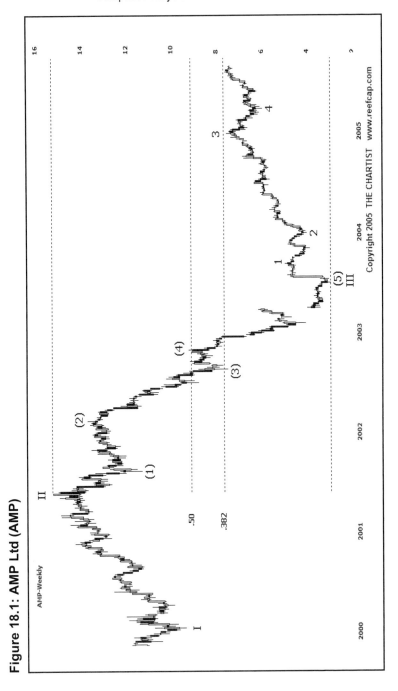

CHAPTER 19

AUSTRALIAN STOCK EXCHANGE LTD (ASX)

ASX remains in a very bullish trend. As can be seen in figure 19.1, the chart suggests prices are in a larger wave (3). Within that pattern, a smaller wave five can be seen to be forming. While a minor setback should be expected over the next 12 months, as the wave (4) runs its course, this will simply represent part of the ebb and flow of the larger price action and could offer an excellent opportunity for the patient active investor. The $19.00 to $20.00 zone should halt that decline, and any break of $16.00 would invalidate the analysis completely.

Adaptive Analysis for Australian Stocks

Figure 19.1: Australian Stock Exchange Ltd (ASX)

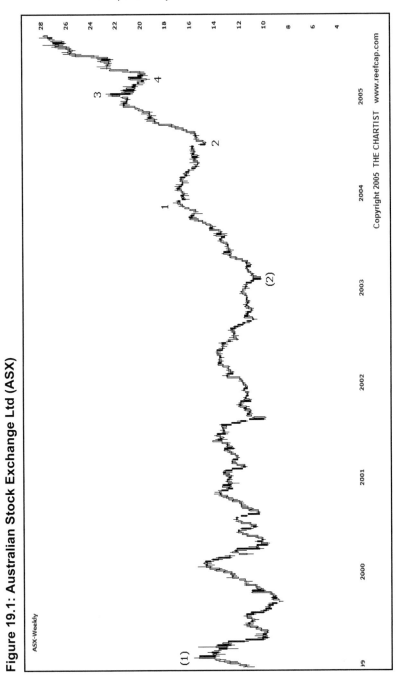

ASX-Weekly

Copyright 2005 THE CHARTIST   www.reefcap.com

CHAPTER 20

BABCOCK & BROWN LTD (BNB)

As can be seen in figure 20.1, BNB is certainly forming a powerful trend in 2005, which came off a perfect A-B-C corrective wave (2). My current interpretation is that this strength represents the impulsive wave (3), but the main question is, 'Where will it stop?' The use of Fibonacci extensions can give some indication. The distance from the list price to the top of wave (1) was $3.70. Under normal circumstances where the waves are nicely proportioned, wave (3) will usually end at a multiple of 0.618 of the length of wave (1). As shown in the chart, though, prices have gone well through that point and are now nearing the 1.618 multiple, which comes in at $17.28. I would expect that after wave (3) is completed, the usual wave (4) will follow but then only a minor wave (5). This is because experience suggests that after a powerful third wave such as this, the fifth wave tends to be weak. Ultimately, the chart remains bullish for the longer term, but I would not be surprised to see a reasonable dip in the interim.

Figure 20.1: Babcock & Brown Ltd (BNB)

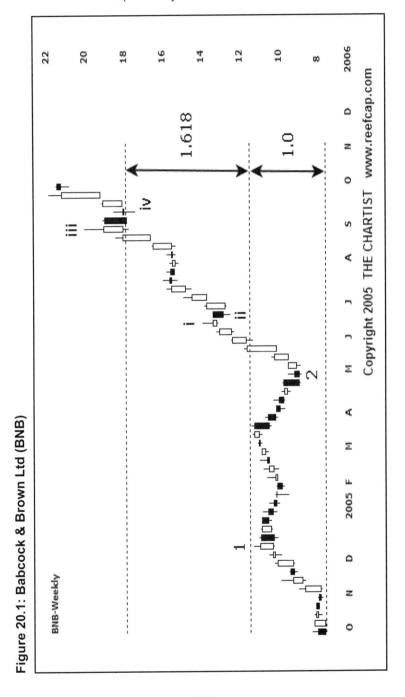

BNB-Weekly

Copyright 2005 THE CHARTIST www.reefcap.com

CHAPTER 21

BLUESCOPE STEEL LTD (BSL)

The powerful trend in the price action of BSL since 2003 extended wave three and subdivided into a smaller five-wave pattern, as shown in figure 21.1. The strong price action seen over the last few years is now correcting in an A-B-C, wave-four pattern. The current strength certainly appears to be a wave B. If this analysis holds true, holders of the stock should be prepared for a reasonable dip in prices over the coming six months or so. Any sizeable dip would be construed as a wave four before another major leg higher.

Figure 21.1: Bluescope Steel Ltd (BSL)

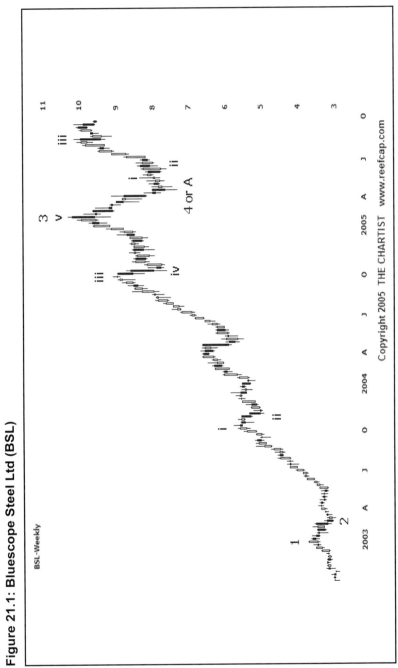

CHAPTER 22

CABCHARGE
AUSTRALIA LTD (CAB)

After a few years in the wilderness through 2001 and 2002, CAB has pushed to new highs with price action, following the rules of EW nicely, as shown in figure 22.1. The triangle pattern that formed during the recent small corrective period suggests the current analysis is valid and that wave five is now under way. The good proportion shown on the chart tilts the probabilities towards further upside, targeting between $6.00 and $6.50. It's probably not the best buying opportunity at the moment, so a patient investor may wish to wait until this pattern is completed.

Figure 22.1: Cabcharge Australia Ltd (CAB)

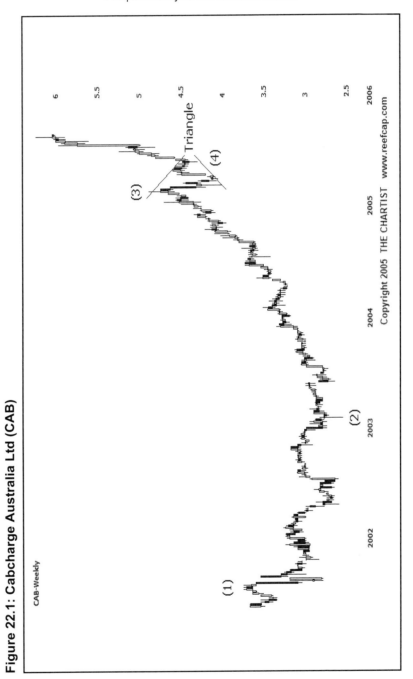

CAB-Weekly

CHAPTER 23

COMPUTERSHARE LTD (CPU)

Prices for CPU are slowly moving higher after a massive collapse between 2000 and 2002, as shown in figure 23.1. The turnaround is tracing out a well-proportioned pattern where the current strength indicates a fifth wave is under way that should take prices closer to $9.00 over the coming 12 months. This wave five could be subdividing into another pattern, as the previous wave three did. If this is the case, the smaller pattern is currently in wave iii.

Figure 23.1: Computershare Ltd (CPU)

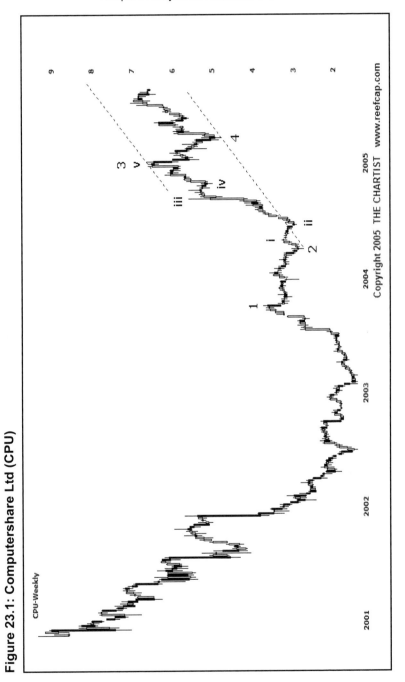

CHAPTER 24

COFFEY INTERNATIONAL LTD (COF)

Like many stocks, COF got its bullish steam in mid-2003 when it broke out of a large basing pattern, as shown in figure 24.1. After an initial retest of that breakout, prices moved higher in a strong impulsive third wave. Current strength is part of the fifth wave and may be drawing to a close, meaning pursuing the stock here does not place the probabilities in the favour of an EW trader. If prices do make a major fifth-wave top, a large corrective move may ensue, which would provide a better buying opportunity.

Figure 24.1: Coffey International Ltd (COF)

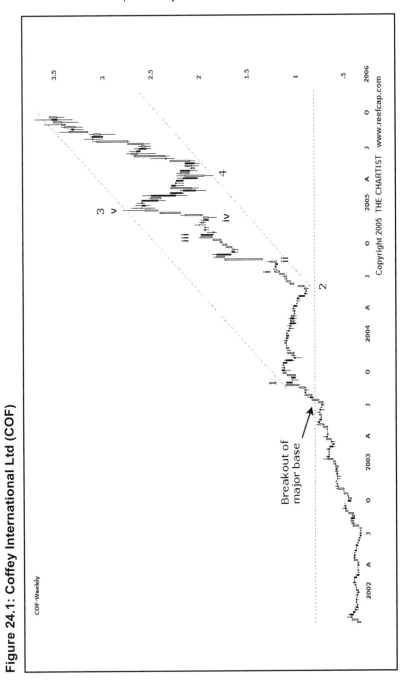

COF-Weekly

Breakout of major base

Copyright 2005 THE CHARTIST   www.reefcap.com

CHAPTER 25

ENERGY DEVELOPMENTS LTD (ENE)

The price action for ENE over 2005 has been difficult to discern, as shown in figure 25.1. The spike in early August 2005 is cause for minor concern, especially if the minor low at $3.77 is breached. This would suggest that the spike will become the larger wave-three high and prices will continue to correct in a wave five. I'd be more tempted to stand aside here and let prices resolve themselves into a more confident pattern. Ultimately, however, the price action remains in a firm bullish uptrend.

Figure 25.1: Energy Developments Ltd (ENE)

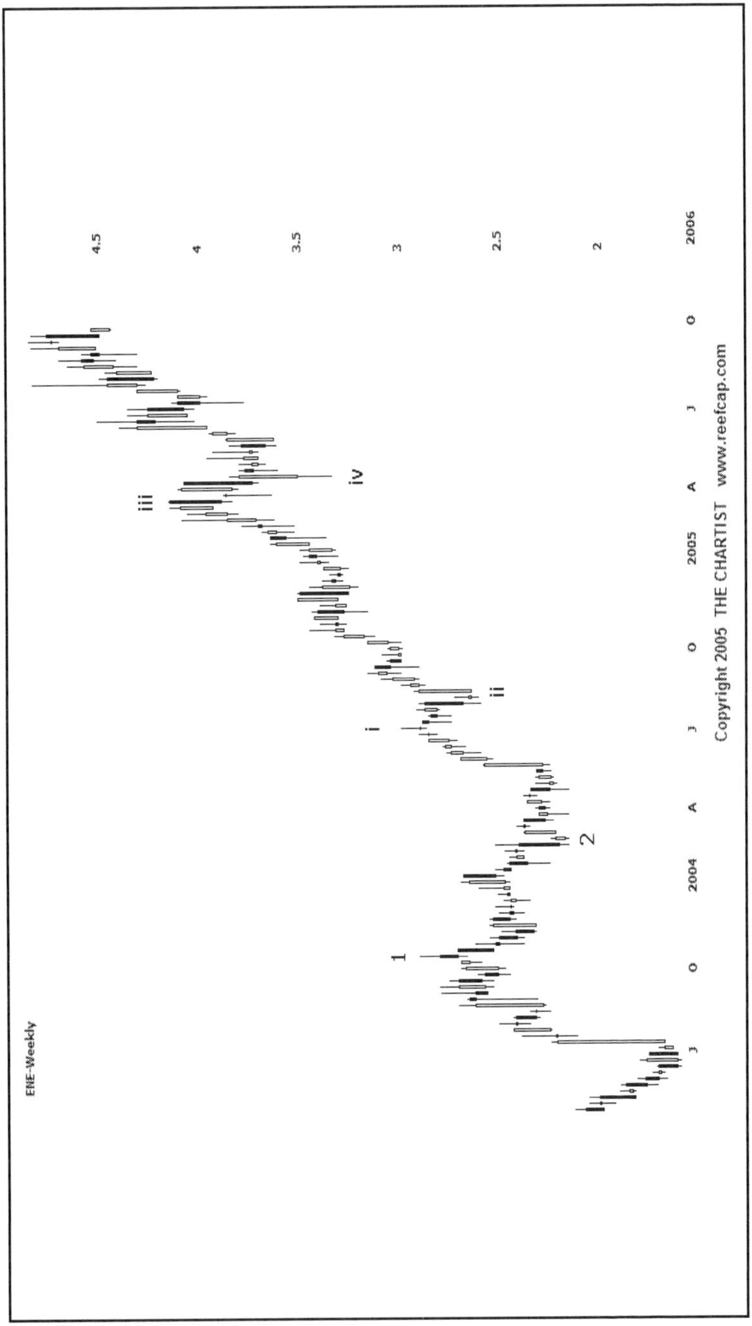

ENE-Weekly

CHAPTER 26

MACARTHUR COAL LTD (MCC)

As you can see in figure 26.1, the price action for MCC has been very dramatic over a very short period of time. If the large ascending triangle marked on the chart is breached on the topside, the resulting price move may be explosive. Prices are coiling in anticipation. There are three clear waves up to form this triangle, and this congestion may well be wave four. Time will tell, but certainly a very bullish chart at the moment.

Figure 26.1: Macarthur Coal Ltd (MCC)

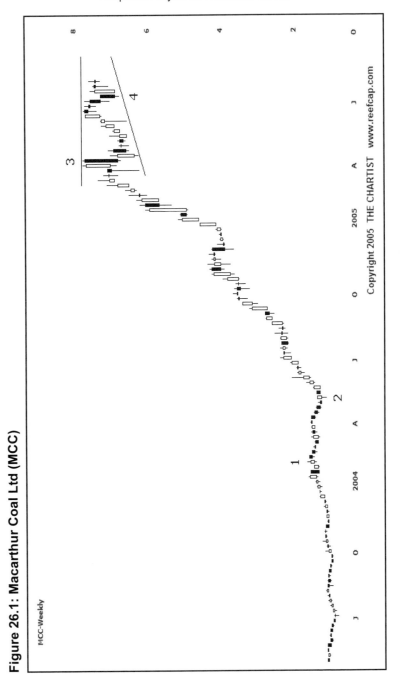

MCC-Weekly

Copyright 2005 THE CHARTIST www.reefcap.com

CHAPTER 27

PUBLISHING AND BROADCASTING LTD (PBL)

The strong price action seen in PBL over the last few years has run out of legs and has moved into a longer term corrective move, as shown in figure 27.1. While prices may probe higher over the c oming months, as wave B is formed, I am sceptical that 2004 highs will be breached before prices move lower. The April 2005 lows, labelled on the chart as wave A, should be breached after any failure of the current strength. That said, the very long-term picture is bullish. Better buying opportunities should present themselves eventually to the patient investor.

Figure 27.1: Publishing & Broadcasting Ltd (PBL)

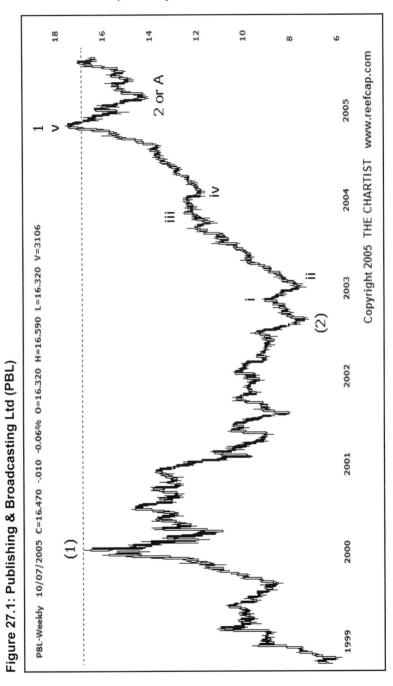

PBL-Weekly 10/07/2005 C=16.470 -.010 -0.06% O=16.320 H=16.590 L=16.320 V=3106

Copyright 2005 THE CHARTIST www.reefcap.com

CHAPTER 28

SALLY MALAY
MINING LTD (SMY)

The last three years have seen a dramatic rise in prices for SMY, culminating in the end of the trend at $1.12 in early 2005, as shown in figure 28.1. My analysis suggests that this high completed a wave five and to date has been followed by the expected wave (A). The strength seen over the last few weeks, as the price moved from $0.75 to $0.85, is part of wave (B). While this may continue, you need to be cautious. Wave (B) will be most likely be followed by a wave (C), forming a new wave (2). As second waves tend to be deeper, future declines can be expected toward the 0.50 to 0.618 levels. Very large confluence can be seen at the 0.618 level, as this is the high of the smaller degree wave one and the low of the smaller degree wave four. If prices are seen in this area, an opportunity for the next large move higher may present itself.

Figure 28.1: Sally Malay Mining Ltd (SMY)

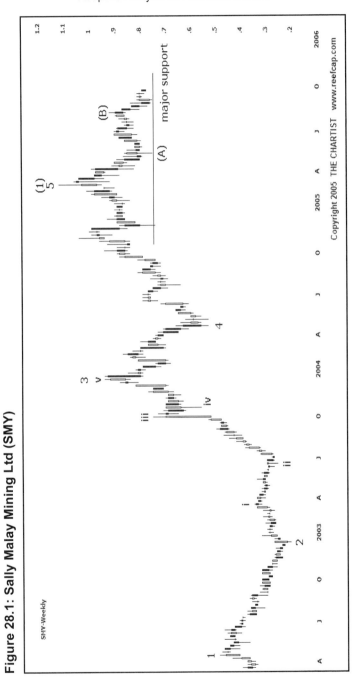

SMY-Weekly

Copyright 2005 THE CHARTIST www.reefcap.com

APPENDIX A

STOPS AND LONG TRADING

The table overleaf outlines what impact the size of the protective stop used will have on results. The number of points used as the protective stop was tested between one and 50, and no other risk management factors were used. The computer was told to buy at every open and close at the end of each day — or get stopped out at the various protective stop loss levels. The exercise shows that a tighter stop may have a smaller win percentage and profitability, but the associated risk declines at an even faster rate — making a tighter stop a better alternative than a wider stop.

Stop points	Net profit	Profit (%)	Avg. win/loss	Avg. trade	Max. drawdown	Profit factor
1	94 900	6	23.26	37.87	−14 550	1.55
2	92 400	10	10.99	36.87	−16 825	1.28
3	100 175	15	6.82	39.97	−26 025	1.22
4	114 575	19	4.92	45.72	−29 425	1.20
5	135 125	24	3.77	53.92	−27 875	1.20
6	147 375	27	3.09	58.81	−30 225	1.19
7	128 875	31	2.56	51.43	−35 025	1.15
8	116 075	34	2.16	46.32	−37 825	1.12
9	98 450	36	1.91	39.29	−42 525	1.10
10	104 150	38	1.74	41.56	−41 200	1.10
11	106 150	40	1.59	42.36	−42 350	1.10
12	83 000	42	1.46	33.12	−51 650	1.07
13	71 675	43	1.37	28.6	−46 050	1.06
14	79 175	45	1.29	31.59	−43 325	1.07
15	71 450	46	1.24	28.51	−45 325	1.06
16	51 275	46	1.19	20.46	−42 775	1.04
17	41 425	47	1.15	16.53	−50 325	1.03
18	34 575	47	1.12	13.8	−47 125	1.03
19	47 025	48	1.10	18.76	−51 650	1.04
20	60 850	49	1.09	24.28	−53 825	1.05
21	52 875	49	1.08	21.1	−54 650	1.04
22	51 600	49	1.07	20.59	−54 400	1.04

Stop points	Net profit	Profit (%)	Avg. win/loss	Avg. trade	Max. drawdown	Profit factor
23	46 800	49	1.06	18.68	−54 725	1.04
24	41 775	49	1.05	16.67	−55 675	1.03
25	43 225	49	1.04	17.25	−57 175	1.03
26	52 200	49	1.04	20.83	−53 850	1.04
27	41 200	49	1.04	16.44	−56 050	1.03
28	45 950	50	1.03	18.34	−49 025	1.03
29	52 950	50	1.04	21.13	−47 450	1.04
30	55 025	50	1.04	21.96	−47 675	1.04
31	60 525	50	1.04	24.15	−47 575	1.05
32	66 200	50	1.04	26.42	−47 625	1.05
33	64 050	50	1.04	25.56	−48 725	1.05
34	59 600	50	1.04	23.78	−48 075	1.05
35	55 775	50	1.03	22.26	−49 325	1.04
36	52 775	50	1.03	21.06	−49 675	1.04
37	51 675	50	1.03	20.62	−49 750	1.04
38	47 975	50	1.02	19.14	−49 850	1.04
39	48 825	50	1.02	19.48	−50 775	1.04
40	47 375	50	1.02	18.9	−49 975	1.04
41	51 675	50	1.03	20.62	−50 375	1.04
42	53 250	50	1.03	21.25	−49 225	1.04
43	55 500	50	1.03	22.15	−49 600	1.04
44	55 425	50	1.03	22.12	−49 975	1.04

Stop points	Net profit	Profit (%)	Avg. win/loss	Avg. trade	Max. drawdown	Profit factor
45	53 900	50	1.03	21.51	–49 825	1.04
46	49 600	50	1.02	19.79	–49 900	1.04
47	54 900	50	1.03	21.91	–50 125	1.04
48	54 050	50	1.03	21.57	–49 375	1.04
49	54 175	50	1.03	21.62	–49 525	1.04
50	50 850	50	1.02	20.29	–49 675	1.04

APPENDIX B

STOPS AND SHORT TRADING

The following table is the inverse of the table presented in appendix A — that is, short selling on every open, closing the trade at the end of each day, or getting stopped out at the various protective stop loss levels. The results from this short selling strategy show very similar characteristics to those in appendix A. You can see, however, that as the stop is widened the profitability drops dramatically, which suggests the upward bias of the stock market over the longer term. My research suggests that short selling strategies for stock markets are only profitable over very short time intervals and have poor results when longer time frames are used.

Stop points	No. of trades	Net profit	Profit (%)	Avg. win/loss	Avg. trade	Max. drawdown	Profit factor
1	2506	67500	6	19.92	26.94	–13425	1.40
2	2506	49300	11	9.30	19.67	–28925	1.15
3	2506	101750	16	6.07	40.60	–35250	1.22
4	2506	84125	20	4.44	33.57	–29475	1.15
5	2506	80425	24	3.42	32.09	–28650	1.12
6	2506	62600	28	2.78	24.98	–25725	1.08
7	2506	67925	31	2.34	27.10	–26600	1.08
8	2506	67425	34	2.01	26.91	–25050	1.07
9	2506	77175	37	1.78	30.80	–28875	1.08
10	2506	87300	40	1.62	34.84	–30300	1.09
11	2506	97275	42	1.48	38.82	–31050	1.09
12	2506	94025	44	1.38	37.52	–31950	1.09
13	2506	82100	45	1.29	32.76	–31075	1.07
14	2506	70700	46	1.22	28.21	–33500	1.06
15	2506	60575	47	1.17	24.17	–35225	1.05
16	2506	40000	47	1.13	15.96	–40425	1.03
17	2506	27850	48	1.09	11.11	–45200	1.02
18	2506	10400	48	1.06	4.15	–60150	1.01
19	2506	18225	49	1.04	7.27	–63550	1.01
20	2506	19675	49	1.03	7.85	–62925	1.02
21	2506	19275	50	1.01	7.69	–63900	1.02
22	2506	9125	50	0.99	3.64	–66800	1.01

Stop points	No. of trades	Net profit	Profit (%)	Avg. win/loss	Avg. trade	Max. drawdown	Profit factor
23	2506	10950	50	0.99	4.37	−63200	1.01
24	2506	−150	50	0.97	−0.06	−72150	1.00
25	2506	−12250	50	0.96	−4.89	−82675	0.99
26	2506	−22750	50	0.95	−9.08	−90425	0.98
27	2506	−28250	50	0.94	−11.27	−92900	0.98
28	2506	−32525	51	0.94	−12.98	−94275	0.98
29	2506	−28700	51	0.94	−11.45	−95100	0.98
30	2506	−23275	51	0.93	−9.29	−90025	0.98
31	2506	−32225	51	0.93	−12.86	−98800	0.98
32	2506	−35400	51	0.92	−14.13	−103425	0.97
33	2506	−34100	51	0.92	−13.61	−100525	0.97
34	2506	−41150	51	0.92	−16.42	−105900	0.97
35	2506	−50275	51	0.91	−20.06	−113125	0.96
36	2506	−53875	51	0.91	−21.5	−117400	0.96
37	2506	−56325	51	0.91	−22.48	−123300	0.96
38	2506	−61500	51	0.90	−24.54	−126425	0.95
39	2506	−59925	51	0.90	−23.91	−124375	0.96
40	2506	−58150	51	0.90	−23.2	−122500	0.96
41	2506	−61025	51	0.90	−24.35	−123925	0.96
42	2506	−56750	51	0.90	−22.65	−119400	0.96
43	2506	−57325	51	0.90	−22.88	−118600	0.96
44	2506	−62175	51	0.90	−24.81	−122325	0.95

Stop points	No. of trades	Net profit	Profit (%)	Avg. win/loss	Avg. trade	Max. drawdown	Profit factor
45	2506	−67 450	51	0.89	−26.92	−126 725	0.95
46	2506	−65 075	51	0.90	−25.97	−124 225	0.95
47	2506	−67 275	51	0.89	−26.85	−125 475	0.95
48	2506	−58 650	51	0.90	−23.4	−115 975	0.96
49	2506	−61 475	51	0.89	−24.53	−118 075	0.96
50	2506	−57 800	51	0.90	−23.06	−115 900	0.96

BANG FOR BUCK INDICATOR

The Bang for Buck indicator can be programmed into various software platforms for easy referral when browsing your trading charts. The coding below has been provided by third parties and no guarantee can be given on the accuracy of this coding.

TradeStation/SuperCharts

Inputs: AvgLength(200);
Plot1 ((10000/(Close))*(Average(Range, AvgLength))/100);

Metastock

((10000/C)* (Mov(ATR(1),200,S))/100)

Amibroker

```
SetOption("InitialEquity",10000);
E = Equity(1);
BFD = E/C*ATR(200)/100;
Plot( BFD, "Bang for $$", colorRed, styleLine );
```

INDEX

Also by Nick Radge

We often hear about the successes of high-flying traders and investors. But rarely do we get an insight into the lives of every-day traders here in Australia, people who often started out with a small amount of money and limited investment knowledge, and, through continuing education and hard work, have managed to carve out a living in the markets.

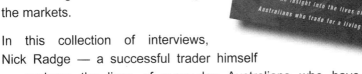

In this collection of interviews, Nick Radge — a successful trader himself — explores the lives of every-day Australians who have traded regularly and profitably for a number of years. Through the detailed questions and answers, he provides insight into the traders' personalities and methods. The issues discussed include:

- trading systems and statistics
- how to approach risk
- entry and exit techniques
- technical and fundamental analysis
- the psychology of trading.

Nick Radge also discusses with interviewees the lifestyle that goes with trading, how they became involved in the sharemarket and what they think it takes to succeed. While the traders interviewed focus on different areas of the markets and use differing tactics, a common theme emerges — that, with discipline and a business-like approach, trading can be a stimulating and financially rewarding journey. You may even get the occasional day off to go surfing!

Published by and available from Wrightbooks,
an imprint of John Wiley & Sons Australia, Ltd